MONEY MANAGEMENT

ERASE DEBTS WHILE INCREASING YOUR WEALTH WITH THIS ALMOST UNKNOWN RULE USED BY THE NEW RICH

LEEROY LINGIBE

CONTENTS

INTRODUCTION

Many people make a lot of money but don't know how it goes. You receive your salary, and after the withdrawals, you realize that you no longer have any in the bank. Your bank account is emptied as if a cyclone had taken there. You no longer understand anything and wonder how you spent your salary. Managing your money well requires discipline in your finances. It's a new way of life that you need to integrate into the way you spend money.

It is worthy to note that bad relationships with money can lead to financial depression. When you want to manage your money to get rich, you give money to the place it deserves in your life. Many people want to maximize money and believe that by earning more money, they will become wealthy. It is untrue, and there is evidence that people who earn very little money with practical money management skills end up being much more prosperous than those who struggle to make a lot ofmoney.

If you wanted to manage your money well, you have to give money in its real place. It is not your money to lead you and push you into compulsive shopping. You are the one who spends your time making money, and it is yours that has the right to direct your income. By having healthy relationships with money, you can manage and control it well.

Sometimes our love for money is not a good thing as it can lead to financial depression. When you don't like money, it's hard to part with it to produce it. The goal in life is not to have the most stocked bank account in the world. So there is no point in maximizing money to prove that you knew how to make money. When you know how to manage your money well, you don't have to earn much to get rich. Money is important, but it should never take the most prominent place in your time.

In our current society, either you're a parent, with a family to take care of, or a single person, you've got huge financial problems. You're always facing tough months' endings, month after month, years after years, and you're going paycheck to paycheck, debts after debts, you're struggling to pay your rent, your car, your kids' hobbies, your basic needs, and many more.

You just can't handle it anymore, and you don't want this life for yourself or your kids…

In this book, I'll share with you my new knowledge after countless years of experience and reading several bestsellers that show how to manage your budget well. If these tips help me manage my money better, they will do the same for you.

What is the Main Solution?

The primary solution will be the 50/30/20 rule, which has been extensively discussed in this book by providing you the best experience you could have, and the best value you could take away from this book. Thus, I'll show you surprising ways to save money, pay off debts effectively, understand the difference between need and want, and then how to manage your budget thanks to this remarkable understanding.

My name is Leeroy Lingibe, and all my childhood, I've been used not to get whatever I wanted, seeing all my friends with brand new shoes or games, that I couldn't have, because of the lack of money of my parents. Not because they didn't have money, they were working, they had more or less a regular salary and consistently, but they couldn't manage it properly. We often got into financial trouble because of it, and obviously, my sisters and I were involved. So I've decided to take their mistakes as a strength when it'd be my turn to handle my own life, and straight away, when I got my first job, and applied this method every single day, and guess what, every single month, without exception, my bank account is still growing and growing. What's giving me the desire to provide you all this knowledge, it's because it's nothing complicated at all. I'm not a banker, and I didn't even study … so if I did it, every single person could escape the trap into the society want to put us in.

Once you are familiar with this system, you'll be able first to reduce all the stress that money can provide, and then live your daily routine in a peaceful mind, you'll start getting more positive, and you'll spread this positivity around you. But financially, you'll also be able to increase your goals, because you'll you won't have to worry anymore about your debts and how to finish the month. Now, you'll be dealing with rich problems which are, how can I make MORE money, and be able to become rich.

From my humble beginnings, I am now at this part of the process, and I've been able to travel in 4 different countries in 3 months, only thanks to this efficient budget management technique.

With my help and expertise, you will be fully equipped with the skills and knowledge you need to change your life in the long-term vision literally. Also, you'll understand the fact that you don't have to become a slave to your money, as it can harm your well-being. Just make it easier for money to prioritize, but don't make money a priority. Managing your money well daily means putting it at your service.

Money is simply a lever in your life, and it allows you to activate your priorities to live comfortably. It's there for you to live the life you want, not the other way around. By developing healthy relationships with your money, you will never be seen as a stingy. People will respect you for what you are and not for what you do. If you put yourself in the service of money, it can destroy your mind. So, you'll understand how to make money as a tool that can serve you.

You don't want to wait anymore; you don't want to raise your debts months after months because the more your waiting, the more difficult it'll be to change the trend. Start this fantastic transformation today and enjoy it for the rest of your life.

Every chapter in this book will provide you with actionable steps that will help you to be in control of your budget and control of your life. If you're applying all the tips and rules in this book, it is very likely that you will never have to take care of your money anymore.

Sit, relax, and enjoy the reading…

1

THE 50%, 30%, 20% RULE

Do you want to erase debts while increasing your wealth with this almost unknown rule used by the newly rich to manage their money? Of course, this is an amazing rule that gives you the right direction you need to increase your wealth. It is the 50/30/20 rule. This rule allows you to distribute your money according to the type of expenditure: such a percentage of your money will go towards such type of expenditure, and so on. I'll teach you in this chapter what you need to understand about this rule and easy ways to set up the 50/30/20 rule.

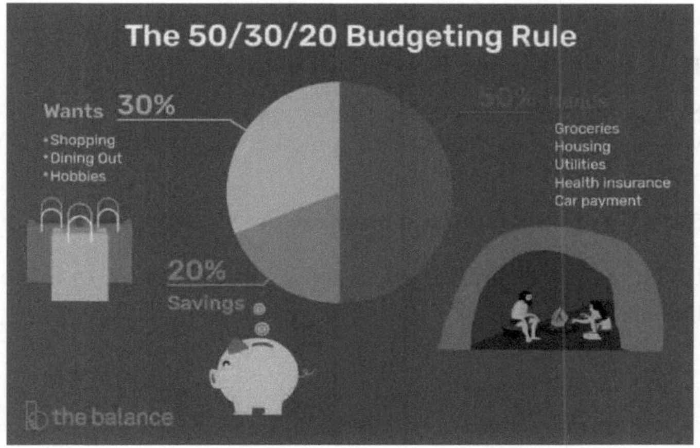

Image by © The Balance 2019

This rule makes it possible, using percentages, to allocate a budget according to the type of expenditure. The 50 represents the percentage of needs and vital expenses not to be exceeded, and the 30 represents the percentage of wants related expenses not to be exceeded either. Finally, 20 represents the percentage of savings to be set aside.

Example: An employee earns $1,500 / month.
50% of necessary expenses = $750 maximum to allocate to this type of expense.
30% for leisure = $450 maximum to allocate to this type of expenditure.
20% for savings = $300 minimum to allocate to your savings.

He must, therefore, spend a maximum of $750 / month for his expenses, $450 / month for his wants (leisure activities), and save at least $300 / month.

How to Implement The 50/30/20 Rule?

Now with this example, you have understood this rule. So we will see how to put it into practice and define where the spending goes.

50% Needs (of vital and compulsory expenses)

Living expenses are all the expenses that we have to make to live each month:

- The rent. Food.
- Electricity. Insurance. Taxes.
- Transportation costs.
- All direct debits.
- Internet and telephone subscriptions.

So be careful not to exceed 50% to stay in the nails. To find out how far you are, just add up all your charges. You can do this on a budget management application online.

For example, thanks to this type of application, you have a vision of all your expenses, and you can categorize them quickly. So you quickly see whether or not you exceed 50%. You can also use one of your bank statements; all your expenses are noted there. Have a view for at least 3 months and average your expenses. Indeed, depending on the month, some expenses may vary, especially for everything related to food. Once you have your expenses, you will simply add them up, and this should not exceed 50%. Here is the calculation to calculate the percentage:

$(100 \times 1150) / 2300 = 50\%$

If you're not good at calculating, just tell yourself that 50% is half your income. So, if you earn $2300, you should not exceed $1150. By adding your expenses, you will quickly see if you have exceeded or not these 50%.

30% of Wants (leisure-related expenses)

These are all the expenses we make to make us happy:
- vacation,
- restaurant,
- visits (amusement park, zoo ...),
- shopping (clothes, decoration…),
- subscription to the sports hall (considered as want).

Again, you will look at your bank statements or your budget management application. You will do the same calculation:

(100 x 690) / 2300 = 30%

If you're not good at calculating, just tell yourself that 30% is 3 × 10%. Knowing that 10% (that is to say a tenth), that's $230, so you have to make 230 x 3 = $690.

Needs Vs. Wants

First of all, know that not recognizing the difference between need and want is very common in the society in which we live. It is not uncommon to confuse the meaning of these two concepts, but what you may not know is that not being able to make a difference can directly impact your life and make you unhappy. Differentiating need and want is essential, and that is why I've decided to share this with you and explain to you what is the difference between need and want.

Needs Are Natural and Necessary

Let's start by giving you an explanation of the concept of need, which, as stated above, is very often confused with want. Here are some characteristics specific to the need and a few examples that will allow you to distinguish it from want immediately. The need is:

- Natural and necessary Goal
- Almost identical from one person to another Limit
- Sometimes fatal if not satisfied: non-satisfaction can lead to death
- Mainly physiological

In everyday life, it is not uncommon at all to hear the sentence: "I need a vacation" or "I need to change my mind." Big confusion here ... Indeed, you do not have the necessary need for a vacation, but the natural need to rest. Taking a vacation is, therefore, only the means of satisfying your natural need, but in no way represents this need.

Just like when you say or hear sentences like, "I need this TV, I absolutely have to buy it!"

No. You do not need this TV; you want to own it, buy it to fill the want. Still, the fact of not having it will have no consequences on your mental, emotional, or physical life, while a need is necessary for our physical, mental, and/or emotional survival.

Wants are fleeting and infinite

Let's continue with a small definition and some examples of wants.

Here we are in having material possession. It about wants, so something I can do without. The dissatisfaction of my want will generate more or less frustration, but we are only here in frustration. Sometimes transient sadness too, but our mental, emotional, or physical life is not at stake.

Some characteristics, the want is:

- Unnatural and fleeting
- Subjective
- Linked to context, place, society, culture, time
- Infinite
- Insatiable. Barely satisfied, he reappears.
- Predominantly psychological

Some examples to illustrate this notion:

When you are thirsty, you need to drink to quench it and provide for a basic need. However, whether you quench your thirst with water or apple juice, it is no longer need but want. Want is a luxury; it involves consciousness, representation, and imagination. Want is a promise of pleasure; this is why want and pleasure are intimately linked, and it is also one of the reasons that lead us to confuse these two notions.

Want is not only superficial and superfluous, but it is also about asserting oneself, one's personality, and a form of freedom. Man is no longer content to provide for his biological needs and necessities. Want is on the side of the spirit; it is predominantly psychological; it develops according to the society in which we live, according to the era, the culture. We can clearly say that want is to culture what need is to nature.

It should be noted that needs are a stronger motivation factor. Indeed, without the satisfaction of many of them, the body is not at all able to exist. At the same time, often receiving what is necessary is taken for granted and does not cause special emotions. At the same time, when fulfilling wants, often having nothing to do with the question of survival, a person can feel himself at the peak of happiness.

Hence, the fact that the number of needs is limited. They exist beyond the will of man and are not positive or negative. Meanwhile, wants, representing a product of the mind, are endless. They can arise as long as there is enough imagination. Nevertheless, wants are controlled, and it is important to be able not to think about something transcendent, but rather rejoice at what is now.

20% Savings

Unlike other types of expenses, this 20% is a minimum. The more you can save, the better:

- life insurance,
- a retirement savings plan,
- A booklet.

This saving can be used to pay off your debts, buy a car, etc. For my part, I split savings into 2 axes: fixed savings and mobile savings. Of the 20% that you are going to save, I advise you to leave half of it on supports on which you will be able to withdraw the money quickly and the other half on media where the money is more or less blocked, such as the life insurance.

How to Respect the Rule?

Once you can identify the amount you've spent on each type of expense, you will have to follow the length rule. I'll give you some techniques for doing this.

Pay for Wants in Cash

Most expenses are fixed; that is, they do not vary from month to month. The expenses that can vary and weigh on your budget are wants and shopping. A good way to stay within your budget for these expenses is to withdraw the money. By paying in cash, you have the money in your hands, so it's more substantial, and you realize your expenses more easily than with a bank card. Indeed, when we pay with the bank card, sometimes we do not even see the amount, and it is even worse with contact- less payment! Sometimes, we also throw the receipt, and we lose it. Above all, the payment intervenes on your accounts sometimes up to 1 week after! This means that if, for example, you forgot the purchase you just made, and a few days later, you buy something else, it may contribute to breaking your budget. With cash, you can see where your budget is from day-to-day.

Buy Your Groceries at The Drive

Honestly, since I did that, my shopping budget has always been the same except for a few dollars. Indeed, by buying at the drive, you almost always buy the same thing. In addition, you are not tempted to buy anything else, and your children do not ask you to buy the whole store and icing on the cake, you save a lot of time since your basket is registered! So you can do your shopping in one click: you no longer go to the supermarket, you just have to take them out and take them home.

Set Up Automatic Transfers for Your Savings

Very often, we tend to save at the end of the month. Except that at the end of the month, there is not much left. To meet the 20% savings target, it would be better to set up a direct deposit. Imagine that your salary arrives on the 5th of the month: you will set up 2 automatic transfers, so you will not need to think about it every month and above all, you will not forget it. Half will go to your fixed savings and the other half to mobile savings.

What Are the Advantages of This Rule?

The advantages of this rule include; it is very easy to understand, the calculations are straightforward to set up, and once the method is set up, you no longer need to look at your accounts regularly. This rule also allows you to please yourself since 30% of your expenses are allocated to wants. Ultimately, you will be able to classify each type of expenditure between the 3 categories: needs/wants/savings.

The Limits of This Rule

According to some financial experts, this rule allows you to start getting started with budget management. Still, it is not a sophisticated method in the long term to manage your budget properly. Indeed, to manage your budget properly, you must know how to calculate your budget, list all your expenses, reduce your expenses, etc. This requires more work, and you also need to be able to control your expenses regularly. There are, therefore, even more advanced methods! Well, this rule effectively allows you to get your foot in the right direction.

The 50/30/20 rule: a bit of history!

This rule was created by Elizabeth Warren, a former Harvard professor now vice president of the United States Senate. It is part of the ranking of the 100 most influential people in the world by TIME magazine.

Your turn! This is an opportunity to test this wonderful rule and experience the best financial lifestyle you've been dreaming of in a lifetime.

2

HOW TO REDUCE AND CONTROL THE "WANTS"

One of the fastest ways to achieve financial freedom is to understand some of the best techniques to reduce and control wants. Also, you need to identify the power of the mind as one of the tools to succeed. For this to work for you, the most important thing here is to understand the principle of the work of a subtle substance called the subconscious, not to be lazy, to be persistent, and to believe in the result.

In this chapter, I'll discuss some of the best approaches to reduce and control wants and also extensively talk about consciousness and the subconscious means of using this situation to achieve your goals by whom and how our subconscious is formed. And also about how to reprogram the subconscious mind, so that as a result, your life will turn out the way you want it to be.

First of all, everyone wants one or two things throughout everyday life, be it another luxury like cars, new telephone, new house, or any other forms of human desire. Most times, we only want things just for "wanting" sake, which can harm our financial balances. Next time you "want" something, inquire as to whether you genuinely want it. On the off chance that you don't, at that point, put it in a safe spot. Life is too short even to consider spending cash on things you don't generally want and won't help you over time.

Generally, we wind up saying, "I want this." While this is superbly typical of most of us, it can be affecting your funds and hurt your financial balances after some time. The following are different ways to prevent you from struggling with your "wants" and "needs":

Distinguish your Triggers

Whenever you go out to get something, be careful, and recognize any triggers that may prompt a hasty purchase. To control your propensities, you should know that they exist—so be informed before they develop into issues—in such a case that you don't check your ways of managing the money, they will never improve.

Learn to Stop

It's difficult to prevent yourself from purchasing some of the things that you want—particularly if you have a feeling that you want them—however, it is something you need to do to keep an idea about your funds. Most people think that its simpler to control their excessive spending as time goes on either weekly, monthly, or yearly. Everybody is unique. In the event that you think that its more straightforward to wind down yourself off exorbitant spending as time goes on, at that point, let it out.

Simply advise yourself that you are progressing in the direction of your objective of a superior spending plan, and utilize that to drive yourself towards an excellent money related future.

Write them Down

Here and there, recording something causes you to see it vividly than contemplating it. For you, at that point, you can begin to write down your considerations and recognize any occasions you feel a "need" to purchase and go through more cash. Begin to distinguish certain feelings with specific triggers, and you will start to shape a relationship for resistance against insignificant spending.

Talk to Somebody

On the off chance that your excessive spending is an issue, share it with somebody that you feel good with. This can assist with diminishing your uneasiness, and somebody with an outside point of view can enable you to recognize what sets you off to spend more—perhaps it is because you are focused or exhausted. Whatever the explanation, discussing any occasions you have an inclination that you "needed" something that you didn't generally need at the time is an extraordinary method to defeat your ways of managing money and develop your budgetary future.

Regarding our mind, conscious and subconscious can be found in mind.

Essentially, the way we approach many things in our daily life all depends on how we think, which is a clear function of the mind. When anyone thinks like a rich person, absolutely he'll surely live in this cycle of thinking while another person thinks with a poverty mindset, then living in this manner is eminent; this is just to emphasize the power of the mind.

But, for this to be precisely the way we need, it is necessary to understand how and by whom our subconscious mind is programmed. Either you can identify this situation or not, you've to know that this is your choice, but the subconscious mind directly affects our desires, goals, thoughts, and actions, as well as on the way to achieve them.

The subconscious mind is a kind of program that is not realized by us, which is inside us. The unconscious formation of which begins from the moment of birth, and continues our whole life.

At first, this happens in the family. The actions, deeds, and words of the parents are perceived by the child as truth, an axiom that does not require proof and is recorded in our subconscious mind as a program for understanding the world.

It is in very early childhood that our attitude to the surrounding reality, an optimistic or distrustful attitude towards people, our outlook on life, certain behavioral stereotypes, habits, and actions are formed.

Just at the beginning of our lives, the tuning and the most real unconscious programming of our subconscious are going on. And, therefore, our further actions, actions, and our lifestyle as a whole will depend on these attitudes.

Not fully understanding the mental processes previously created by external sources, over time, they begin to be embodied in our lives. And what happens to us is what we don't want, but for some reason, we are not able to control these processes.

Why Did It Happen?

This is the work of our so-called programs recorded by parents, kindergarten, school, etc., which are manifested in the image of our unconscious thoughts, actions, and deeds.

It is these programs of the subconscious that give invisible orders that control our life and us. They make us act one way or another in certain situations, guide us in one direction or another in life, and are fully responsible for the wealth, success, and construction of our entire life.

It is also worth saying here that the essence is not only in the programmed belief in our subconscious. However, it is a choice about a stream of everyday information. We are constantly surrounded by ideas, thoughts, and words that affect our well-being, success, and wealth.

After all, everything that surrounds us in our daily lives directly affects us, not only consciously, but subconsciously.

Namely; if, we consciously receive a stream of negative, destructive information. Our subconscious mind will eventually translate this into our reality. For instance, if you read proper, good books, you have happy thoughts. If you read horror books, nine out of ten negative events will happen in your life. When you focus on a piece of news, your brain writes this news as a fact. And this news will affect you, in a good or bad aspect.

Remember one thing.

How you live, what you have, what you do or don't do, what your relationship is, whether you are single or happy, each part of your existence is the result of your thoughts in the past. And it has a direct relationship to the fact that your subconscious mind is recorded from the moment you are born, and to the present moment.

It is essential to note that each of our actions has been programmed before. Each word that you heard from someone you took and consciously placed in your subconscious, for processing. Which, in turn, was processed as a fact, further created a reaction, and was subsequently transferred to consciousness for subsequent execution.

The subconscious programming happens every day with the flow of information that you receive. And here it is important to realize, or ask a question, what type of program we received earlier and continue to receive every day?

If we received good positive thinking in early childhood, we would ultimately become an excellent creative person with a strong character and the right moral principles. But, if from birth, a person receives negative emotions and thinking. Such a person will have low self-esteem and not the ability to show their true skills. As a result, as a rule, he becomes a juvenile delinquent, drug addict, alcoholic, and ultimately his life is completely ruined.

Take, for example, this scenario:

The child was born in a very rich and influential family. This child will be programmed from childhood that money is the most essential thing in this world.

What is most important in life is to have a lot of money. This child is programmed to power all the laws of life; for him, it is concentrated only around cash. Money in his life will always play the most crucial role.

From birth, he received a software installation to value, respect, and use money as a means to achieve any goals in life. He will surely look down on those who do not have money, as his family does. As a rule, such families include those people who have achieved their wealth in a dirty and dishonest way.

Such a program will bring a lot of unhappiness to a person because it leads the child to the idea that rich people are better than anyone in the world. There may be many examples, such as this one, or the opposite.

How many people, so many lives and programs.

But, here, it is simply important to understand that our thinking is not always OUR thinking; it is often not sown by us from birth. Moreover, you may not even be aware of this, because this information is laid in such a way that we do not know that we received it.

The programming of our subconscious mind takes place at an unconscious, subconscious level. That is why it is vital to control your thoughts and information from the outside, every day. And be able to cut off your attention from those aspects that bring irritation and discomfort to your life.

If, in the future, you want to live happily, take care of your reality, most notably regarding your wants. It can be compared to a garden. If you plant roses, but don't take care of them, and leave the garden unattended, what will happen in it?

That's right, weeds will grow among roses in the garden, and beautiful roses will become shrubs. Weeds will grow with plants and may even drown them, absorbing more and more nutrients from the soil.

To avoid this scenario, it's incumbent on you to take care of the garden regularly. A well-tended garden will produce fruits and berries in abundance, and beautiful roses, not weeds, will always be fragrant in it.

This applies to the conscious and subconscious.

If negative thoughts prevail in your mind, these thoughts will be processed in your subconscious. In turn, they will be used as an installation for further reality to be embodied at a certain time.
Therefore, feed your mind only with conscious, constructive, and good thoughts. These thoughts will be processed in the subconscious and remain in memory for the embodiment of the beautiful in your life.

The main thing to remember is one principle.

The subconscious mind does not know what is right or wrong.

It does not know what is good or bad.

It processes only what it receives And that's all it does.

You must be able to control all the subconscious processes of your mind.

Since it is precisely your vigilance and control that can prevent bad thoughts from entering your mind, and protect you from frustration and pain in the future, to reprogram the subconscious, you will have to change your beliefs completely, that is, rewrite attitudes and habits.

To completely change negative thinking into positive, creative, and productive thinking, with the help of which you will know in advance what you need to do to become what you want to be. And then wealth and prosperity will forever enter your life.

This, by the way, can be done very simply. To do this, you just need to learn how to work on yourself and remove all negativity from your life. The best way to change the previous programs already recorded in our subconscious is to replace, that is, reprogram the subconscious with 3 accessible, simple, and effective methods.

All that is needed is diligence and the desire to put your subconscious mind at your service. Completely change all previously recorded programs. Develop new habits and program your life, your worldview, according to your desire. Surely you have already met many available technologies, techniques, methods with which you can reprogram your subconscious.

In the framework of this chapter, I will simply list 3 methods that everyone can apply, and at the same time, quickly get the desired result.

1. Visualization

You must lose, see what you would very much like to have or to realize. To do this, you just need to create various plausible realistic and very desirable life-giving vivid plots or situations. And try to give this picture a positive emotion. And the stronger this emotion and your faith in the credibility of this picture, or image, the faster you can make changes to the old program and write in the subconscious mind a plan to implement this task.

2. Self-hypnosis

This method is aimed primarily at increasing your self-esteem. This is done by repeating the same previously recorded positive qualities and affirmations.

For instance:

You say to yourself every morning and evening: I am rich, successful, smart, slim, healthy, beautiful, strong, etc. In a word, you really should believe in it, and speak with the statement that you are already what you want to be. After 40 days, the subconscious mind will enter these statements into its archive and write this thought into its algorithm to complete the task.

3. Meditation

This is the most effective way of programming the subconscious and gives the best and fastest result. But for its implementation, you will need the ability to concentrate your thoughts and a particular zeal. The technique of meditation works wonders, and if desired, anyone can master it.

During the meditation period, you can not only make adjustments to the subconscious program but also make reality correspond to your desires. Meditation allows you to not only rewrite the program code of the subconscious, and make the necessary changes, but also helps to reveal the true talents in yourself.

Also, with the help of meditation, you can become calm, balanced, healthy, increase vital energy, and direct all mental processes in the direction you need. Of course, these are far from all methods; in reality, there are many of them. But here, it is important to understand that the essence is not in the method, but in patience, perseverance, and the systematic implementation of techniques, plus time. But I want to say, no matter what method you choose to reprogram the subconscious, it will certainly bring results.

Subject to your firm determination, make these changes

If you feel despair and unwillingness, internal coercion, or discomfort from the fact that you need to change something or change. Such an approach will lead to nowhere or give catastrophic results. Better not try to make changes if you do not want to change anything.

But if you have firmly decided that change is necessary, then you will begin to act right now. In this case, reprogramming the subconscious mind will bring you the desired result, and happiness, joy, wealth, success, and everything you need to enjoy life and get everything you want from life will come into your life.

Normal level

It is important to know that each person has a certain level of standard of living. For some, the normal level is a two- room apartment in some small town or village, a refrigerator, and a TV. Someone else needs to add a microwave, surely a spouse, children, so that the dog also exists.

Someone else needs a cottage, a good job, an apartment, or a house in a big city, friends, not just friends, but friends abroad.

"Each person has a certain standard of living to which he is used and which supports."

Take, for example, a rich person who is used to living at a fairly high level. He cannot feel good, for instance, if we are talking about a woman, without a daily manicure. Or, for example, a man who has a house, a Porsche car, a summer house on the Mediterranean coast, a yacht, and so on.

Take away all these things from him that is, artificially lower him this level of the norm of life. And you will see that after a while, everything will return to its circles. He will have everything again because he already has neural connections in a certain way that will again bring him back to his place. This place is called "I just can't do without it." Not only does he already know how to achieve this, but he is also used to it. He cannot strive for this, and without it, he cannot do anything.

Conversely, take the poor man and give him all the wealth that can be given at once. Give him all the wealth of the person from the previous example. After some time, his neural connections, his brain will return him - he will lose everything and will come back again.

"Raise your standard to change your life and take it to a new level of quality of life."

Because the neural connections corresponding to his new life are not stacked in his head. They need to be folded independently, performing certain exercises, and the more often we do this, the stronger these connections will become. It plays into our hands.

Subconscious Exercises

What practices do you need to do to train your brain to put together the right neural connections in our head so that everything works out and everything works out? It is very important to adhere to the concept of "Yin-Yang." It could be decomposed into men and women, but this is wrong because each genus has two sides, Yin and Yang. What is it?

♦ 1 Technique of touching Yang

Yang is a touch technique. You need to think about how your life will change when your desire is fulfilled, what will be new in it? Where will you go? Where will you go? Who will you talk to? How will you dress? What shops, restaurants, cinemas, and so on the go? How can your life change?

Think about how you can now relate to this life. Touch technique - as you can now touch the life that awaits you in the fulfillment of all your desires. Thus, you, as if immersing yourself now in a different atmosphere. You accustom your brain to another life. At first, he will resist, because you will be embarrassed, somehow at ease.

♦ 2 Love Yourself Technique
The one-touch technique is not enough, because it is only one side. It is also essential for you to work on the part of Yin. How to do it better? This technique is called "love your- self." This is a simple and effective technique. And men are also affected. It is very important to approach yourself and your subconscious from the emotional side.

Stop the fuss, stop all the restlessness around you. Actually, stop time, stop yourself, stop your thoughts, all worries. It is very important for you to allocate time for yourself, for your hobby, to come up with some pleasures for yourself, for example, so that no one touches you 1 hour a day. This hour is only yours for your pleasure.

Come up with something for yourself. Buy yourself any gifts, please yourself with some little things, come up with something nice for yourself. Perhaps a restaurant, a beauty salon, an appointment for a massage, a pool, a fitness club, fishing trips, shopping, self-education, yoga, meditation, and so on.

"So that your subconscious mind no longer sabotages you, show love for yourself, reward yourself. And then you will have more energy to achieve any goal."

If in the technique of touching Yang, we approach from the side of the body, as if physically touching our dreams, then in this technique, we are touching the soul, emotions. Thus, you will increase your level of the norm not only at the level of physics but also at the level of emotions. And it turns out such a kind of double blockage of your brain so that it no longer sabotages so that it would be a comfortable, familiar zone for him, and so he would like it.

♦ 3 Wheel of Balance

To understand which direction of the life you should pay more attention to touching Yin, you can beat more accurately at the most lagging areas of your life, so as not to waste energy, to accurately understand in which direction you should pull yourself up.

To do this, you need to perform a simple exercise Wheel Balance. This is a simple exercise, do it, and you will see what and where you are limping, and where you need to add a little of your energy.

The Wheel of Balance is an ordinary circle that you draw on your piece of paper. Imagine a round cake that you cut into 8 parts - this is how you need to divide the circle into 8 sectors. They need to be signed in this way:

1. Everything related to the family and relationships in the family;
2. Your health, what is connected with this (sports, bath, hardening, dietary supplements, fitness, yoga, etc.);
3. Your career;
4. Everything related to finance;
5. Everything related to relationships with other people, with friends;
6. Everything related to your vacation, entertainment, hobbies, travel, that is, for the soul;
7. Personal growth and your self-education;
8. Spirituality, charity, your mission, what benefits do you give the world, people, animals, and so on.

"This simple exercise will help you see where you need to add your energy."

Take these 8 sectors. And go through them, rate them at the moment on a 10-point scale, how much you need to implement each of these areas. Take and put points from 0 to 10.

And you will see what quite important areas of your life that are limping are, and you can already direct your energy there, using the "love yourself" (Yin) technique. You can also use Yang in the same areas.

Thoughts, both positive and negative, can affect lifestyle. There is a simple, effective, and free way to create the ground for the attraction of good luck and financial success thanks to your positive thinking, for which you need to pronounce certain affirmations - statements.

Affirmation for money is a short phrase of a powerful message, forming in the subconscious of its pronouncer a mood for abundance and wealth, motivating for actions, awareness of new ways of making money aimed at a prosperous life.

The Role of Affirmations

The influence of positive good thoughts and emotions on the life of a person, on what is happening around him is enormous. Verbal formulas of affirmation and suggestions are significant for achieving aspirations in many areas of life, accelerating the fulfillment of desires. Affirmations change the negative perception of life into positive, maintaining affirmative attitudes in the human mind: in Latin, affirmation means "confirmation." Their power is tremendous in acquiring financially stable success.

Evidence-based studies by physiologists have shown that words, like signals from the higher nervous system, coming from the brain into the inner world of a person, reconfigure the vital functions of the body for a long time. Speech formulas help the mind to work on a positive wave. Repeated repetition of words reinforces the desired attitude in the human subconscious, improving the psycho-emotional background, causing better changes.

How to make an affirmation for money?

When starting to write verbal formulas, it is important to understand that affirmations for money and success carry a positive statement. In essence, the use of a negative particle is not perceived by consciousness. To achieve an effect in a word, adhere to the rules for compiling affirmations:

The statement is formulated as a fait accompli in the current time. If you say: "I want to be rich," then the subconscious mind understands how: "you want, then continue to want further," and if you say: "I am rich," the answer will be: "you are rich."

The phrase should be short, bright, containing specific images.

You need to choose a formula that suits you specifically.

The statement can be completed as follows: "I will get more than I'm waiting for."

Believe in spoken words.

Affirmations On Wealth

Many want wealth and financial well-being, but internally have obstacles to their achievement. The approval technique is used to reprogram the subconscious for financial success. Affirmations concentrate consciousness on wealth, stimulating them to do something more, revealing as much as possible. They remove the limiting blocks on the path to enrichment, which most have:

- a sense of unworthiness of financial prosperity;
- lack of faith in the ability and ability to make good money;
- fear of taking concrete actions to create material abundance;
- the opinion that money is a source of evil, wealth cannot be achieved through honest labor.

Affirmations for Work and Money

The information received by the mind is processed at the level of the subconscious, which does not distinguish where certain information is and where fantasy is. If you tell your- self that there is not enough knowledge for a career and a big salary, that life is going wrong. The subconscious mind believes this, appropriately regulating all the actions of a person.

If you say affirmatively: "I am a strong and confident specialist with extensive experience, the prospect of career growth, income," naming the desired salary. With the help of affirmation for money and career, everything will start to work out successfully.

Set for money and success

How to become successful and live in wealth? You just need to want this, but first, you need to understand what installations, received in childhood, prevent you from becoming successful. If your parents claimed that it's better to live rather poorly and honestly, and you agreed with them, then under the influence of such an attitude, you won't become a billionaire.

Having identified the problematic definitions, you need to get rid of them. You must name these negative attitudes for you, formulate what you want to have, and then pronounce a phrase like: "I'll delete everything old!" and make a statement that guides you in a successful direction.

Affiliations to attract customers

Many entrepreneurs, beginning and already held, are wondering whether it is possible to make a business effective using the technique of affirmation. A positive attitude preserves the psychological state at work, helping to avoid stress and spreading to other areas of life. Speech formulas, to attract customers, you must form a stream of prosperity and abundance in thoughts. There are certain rules for creating affirmations:

- they should be attractive to customers and buyers; the affirmation must purposefully formulate the desire to attract customers;

- its reading should become familiar;

- repeat the installation as many times a day as you see fit;

- if the affirmation is no longer inspiring, consider a new one;

- you cannot mix affirmations of different goals.

How to Work with Affirmations

Practicing speech settings is simple, but you must follow the rules for their use:

- Make sure affirmation is positive, formulated in the present tense.

- Work with one or two formulas, no more.

- Words can be sung, spoken to oneself, pronounced aloud, written many times on paper, recorded on the browser home page, or saved in audio format.

- A phrase can consist of a couple of words to several sentences.
- Speak affirmations to attract money with an expression.
- Money affirmation is repeated daily, three times a day: in the morning, in the afternoon, and in the evening.

How to pronounce

The affirmation pronounced in front of the mirror when a person looks into his own eyes is a powerful tool! During the repetition, you need to relax as much as possible. The more you concentrate on making the statement, the more notice-able, the faster the result. The pronunciation has a greater effect in a higher voice than the usual tone, while one must speak with a positive feeling, clearly pronouncing each word, without rushing.

Why money-raising affirmations do not work

If you don't feel shifts, the main thing is not to despair! You should not expect a quick miracle if your attitude to finances and wealth has been negative for a long time. Still, many people make typical mistakes when using the technique that interferes with the effect of affirmation:

- doubt, admit negative thoughts;
- mechanically, without emotion read the installation; visualize the desired image, combining the image of desire and pronunciation of the text, not understanding their differences;
- they don't fix the formed habit, quitting the practice within three months, then the old attitudes begin to influence you again.

Top Money Affirmations

To attract money into your life, create affirmations that are comfortable for yourself, or select from the list:

- I magnetize wealth and money.
- I love and choose abundance and wealth, and I feel pleasure from them.
- I have as much money as I want!
- I am worthy of a rich life; I move towards it with confident steps.
- My cash income is growing every day!
- I am a happy, successful, wealthy businessman! Unexpected money flows to me easily and in large quantities.
- I have a good income; my work brings me a lot of money.
- My financial well-being makes me happy.
- I am comfortable with a lot of money.

Our consciousness is not something permanent. It is flexible, and it can be changed, improved, rebuilt. Another thing is that it can take a different amount of time, but here we are almost powerless.

Psychologists say that each person's subconscious mind is unique. Our inner world is bottomless, endless, and beautiful, each in its way. One way or another, but many of our victories are impossible without the right attitude. It is necessary to program yourself for success if only because, in the opposite case, negative virus programs can seize your consciousness, which will drag the rope to the other side - towards failures, ill health, depression, and so on.

Success is an internal struggle

Have you noticed that successful people are successful in almost everything? The reason lies in their mood, and not just in the genes. They won their inner struggle when they dismissed the possibility of failure. Most famous athletes say that they saw their victories long before this became a reality.

Fight negative thoughts so that they do not translate into defeats and failures. No one says that it is easy to go through life with confidence in your victory, but at least you should try. Of course, nothing happens - every success implies at least a small, but a war within each of us. Consciousness builds the world around us. Thoughts are material, so we are as if drawing them on a blank canvas of life. Thoughts are colors, and reality is a sheet of paper.

Without effort, you will have nothing. You need to configure yourself properly and do not forget that only transforming consciousness you transform your life.

3

PAY OFF AND DESTROY YOUR DEBTS FOREVER

From the previous chapter, I've discussed some of the best approaches to adopt in controlling your wants, and we continue the conversation in this chapter with pragmatic ways to pay off and destroy your debts forever.

Today I want to appeal to all those who are drowning in debt. Also, to those who have debts and who believe, with all conviction, that the debts are good. Those who have resigned themselves to living in debt and unable to save money, buy a house, or pay for the car.

If you are being burdened by debt or lack of financial freedom, if you are distressed about not having something to go on vacation with, paying rent, paying for your children's college, and more, this chapter will bring you hope.

There is no magic formula for paying off debts. Today I'm going to give you awesome methods so that you can finally pay off your debts and get used to the idea of living debt-free forever.

Is There Anything Like Good Debts and Bad Debts?

Before we start, I want to tell you something. I, like you, have also been told that not all debts are bad. That there are good debts and bad debts. That you need to take out loans to build your credit history. And that there are things that you always have to finance, such as a car, because no one has the money to buy it in cash.

By the way, to delve into this topic, I'll want you to understand financing a car is one of the worst mistakes you can make with your money.

I have consulted with financial advisers who have advised me to keep my debts. But every time I listen to someone who tells me to live in debt, my stomach turns. I dislike him. What's more, writing about it right now makes me feel uncomfortable.

They Are All Debts

When you decide to listen to your intuition, which is the one that is talking to me when my stomach hurts, just thinking about getting into debt, I realize that it is not natural. So even your body rejects it.

Haven't you noticed? That debts take away your sleep, stress you are not able to pay them, cause conflicts with your partner, and overwhelm you. There is no good feeling that debts produce.

But we eat with salt and pepper this lie that is sold to us in the media and in the society in which we live, in which consumerism is promoted. "Buy everything you want now; it doesn't matter if you have the money to pay for it. Why do you worry about that if you can finance it?"

The credit card offers come to your house every day if they are not talking to CUSTOMER SERVICE representatives, to your house to offer you the new card with miles and points, and I know.

But living in debt is not going to take you down the path of financial freedom; on the contrary, it is going to bind you. As one of the financial experts rightly stated, "Dave Ramsey" puts it well." Your number one tool for accumulating wealth is your income, your salary."

When you have your salary committed to paying the car, the furniture, the children's brakes, the Christmas of 4 years ago that you signed with the card, the mattress, the gum, the gasoline, etc. Everything you sign with the card and that accumulates in the statement because you do not have to pay it, you will never be able to progress financially.

You will never have more than enough to save money, invest, pay your home mortgage, or have a piggy bank for emergencies if you live buying things that you cannot afford today but for which you can cover the monthly "subscription."

Keep or Pay Debts?

From other financial experts that I know Dave Ramsey is the only financial advisor, I've ever heard who promotes this philosophy of living without debt. There are many who, although they have good advice, also tell you that if you have your debts at low interest, keep them. Why? According to them, you can earn more money by investing what you would pay for your debts and earning better interest.

Yes, but this philosophy assumes that you have the money to invest and that, in reality, you are going to invest it, and you are not going to spend it. Assume that every day you will have a job and that you will never face unemployment. This philosophy considers ideal scenarios, but not the reality of our daily lives.

Things happen. For example, you get sick and can't go to work. A loved one dies. You have to change tires on the car. You have a son. So many things happen in our lives that they are far beyond the fantasy scenario in which it would be convenient, mathematically, to invest your money so that it generates more interest than what it costs you to pay for your low-interest debts.

With that said, let's get to know the awesome steps to pay off and destroy your debts forever.

The following are awesome steps to pay off and destroy your debts forever:

Step # 1 Change Your Mindset

The first step to paying off your debts and regain your financial freedom is to change your mindset.

Forget what your neighbor, friend, cousin, sister-in-law tells you, etc. As long as you listen to the versions of why it is wonderful to continue to be in debt, you will never progress. If you want to live better, without debt, then stop thinking that there are good debts and bad debts. They are all debts.

Debts allow you to grow your wealth, for example, when you buy a house. If this house is well cared for, on a desirable course, and you maintain it, this house can grow in value. In the future, you could sell it and generate a good profit.

But if you buy this same house and you don't have money for maintenance, and you don't take care of it, the neighbors are going to start moving. Their home values are going down because yours looks like a haunted house. As a result, the value of that same house decreases.

So stop thinking that there are good debts and bad debts. They are all debts. The faster you get rid of them, whether it's the house or the refrigerator, the more money you will have left in your bank account and the better situation you will be in.

How to Influence the Mind?

Bioenergy specialists and psychologists identify only 5 basic and most effective ways to influence a person on himself. Each method can be used by you separately, but if you use the combination of these techniques, then the chances of success will be even greater.

The first method: affirmations (even though I've extensively discussed this in chapter 2). This is the longest, but very simple way. Its essence consists only in the constant repetition of special motivating phrases. When you tell yourself that you are successful, luck in money itself finds you. Of course, it will take a lot of time to turn negative programs into positive ones, but it will be worth it. This is a flexible way because you can tell yourself anything you want.

You can take advantage of affirmations, there is a simpler option - you can come up with affirmations yourself, in accordance with your requests. Do you need to pay off and destroy your debts forever? Tell yourself, and over time, this will come. The main thing is not to give up. The only minus of affirmations is that you cannot see success clearly because the transition from an unhappy life to a happy one is a long and continuous process.

The second way: positive thinking. There are a lot of sub-items in this technique. For example, you need to get rid of any use of the word "no." It robs you of positive energy, making it difficult to contact the center of the fertility of the universe. Positive thinking also implies the use of several postulates, rules that are similar to affirmations.

Their difference lies only in the fact that they do not require repetition. You just need to take them for truth:

- you can always achieve whatever you want;
- you can pay off and destroy your debts forever;
- everyone forms his happiness.

Think more often about what you want to achieve. If you need to pay off and destroy your debts forever, then think as if it had already happened. If you need a good job, then do not stop searching for it, because there is such a job. You seem to be already happy, but you just haven't reached this point. You are on the way. You can.

Third way: playing sports. You might think that this has nothing to do with the mind, but this is not so. It is not necessary to try to set records or become the strongest. It is enough just to do exercises and not be afraid of physical labor.

According to statistics, people with obesity or health problems due to a sluggish lifestyle achieve success 80% less than active individuals. This also includes bad habits, such as smoking or alcohol abuse. You can drink, smoke too, but you cannot raise this to the degree of necessity. Sometimes everyone wants to relax - there is nothing wrong with that, but you do not need to make the habit control you and draw money from you.

The fourth method: a hobby. Remember that only busy people have a chance of success. Your mindsets in positive when you are doing something pleasant. Let it be embroidery, reading books, watching movies, or something else. It can be anything. Follow your dreams and give your subconscious mind what it wants, but it will not harm you.

Luck in any of the areas of life depends on many factors, but the most important is your attitude. Live as if there is nobody else in this world besides you, but do not forget about loved ones who need your warmth. You can change your fate right now because you have a desire. Let your life be different from this second.

Step # 2 Change Your Behavior

The second step to paying off your debts and regain your financial freedom is to change your behavior.

Do you realize that you are indebted today for the elections you made yesterday? Maybe you decided to take a trip, and since you didn't have all the money, you used your credit card. Maybe you wanted a new car, and instead of buying an old one for cash, you went to finance the 8-cylinder truck of the year. Maybe you bought a house, and to furnish it you bought everything new and modern. Maybe you had liposuction, and you're still paying the card.

Whatever your situation, to pay your debts, it is necessary to realize that you must change your behavior. You must remove the financing option.

And I want to parenthetically here, this rule I think has only one exception. It's about financing a house. As long as the monthly mortgage payment does not exceed 25% of your monthly salary and you have plans to pay it as soon as possible.

Step # 3 Spend Less Than You Earn

The third step to pay off your debts and regain your financial freedom is to spend less than you earn. The only way to prosper financially is by having money. It is such a simple concept that it even sounds absurd. But I am serious.

Get used to spending less than you earn. Because if you have debts, it is a sign that you are not. You get into debt when you spend more than you earn. The formula is simple.

Spending less than what you earn is said easier than it is. In reality, we have many temptations and facilities to get into debt. But if you change your mind, if you force yourself to eliminate the use of credit cards and financing, you are going to give a radical change to your life.

Step # 4 Destroy Your Credit Cards and Eliminate Financing

The fourth step to pay your debts and regain your financial freedom is the one that requires more discipline. You need to destroy the credit cards and stop acquiring new debts. As long as you don't eliminate that temptation, you won't be able to commit to living debt-free. Take out the scissors and cut them. Put them in a paper shredder. Do what you have to do, but remove them from your life.

And if you are about to tell me that you only use them for points and miles, I assure you that sooner or later, you will end up getting into debt and regretting using them.

Step # 5 Make A Budget

To pay off debts, we need to squeeze as much money out of our income as possible and pay it off. The only way to know how much we can pay them is to get accounts with a detailed budget.

Budget Your Expenses

The budget is essential in the debt payment process because it will indicate how much money we have available to feed the beast (the beast is your debts). The more money you squeeze out of your budget to pay for them, the faster you will get out of them.

You will have to make important decisions. If you have a financed car, I recommend that you evaluate the possibility of selling it, paying off that debt, and buying a cheap car that will take you and bring you. In the United States, the average monthly payment for a car over the years was $500 a month, imagine paying that extra to debts!

Sadly, many live clinging to the car they drive. Their vehicle becomes something that defines them, and they would never consider selling it and stopping to ride in an old car. If that's your case, I'm just asking you, what are your priorities? Maintain appearances, or achieve financial freedom and prosper?

Pay Off Debts

With your budget done, you will be able to give an idea of how much money you can pay on debts. Consider canceling the cable, selling your car, saving on the cell phone plan, and canceling unused subscriptions. If you never go to the gym, cancel the subscription. Use that money to pay debts.
Instead, he takes the poor dog out for a walk, locked up at home.

Also, if you are trying to get out of debt, you better prepare your lunch at home. Going to eat with friends after work, to have a beer, or to the movies is also out of your possibilities. You have no money to party. You need to spend an extra penny to pay off your debts. Get down to the rhythm of life that led you to get into debt.

Step # 6 Use The Avalanche Technique to Pay Debts

The objective of the avalanche method is to pay off debts as soon as possible, regardless of the interest rate they have. Once we have our budget done, use the avalanche technique to pay your debts.

This technique consists of making a list of all your debts, from the smallest to the largest. You are going to pay the minimum payment on all your debts. Use the money we squeeze from your budget to pay the smallest until you eliminate it.

Once removed, you will use the amount you were paying in the minimum monthly payment to pay the next debt on the list. We will pay from the smallest to the largest regardless of the interest rate they have.

Pay Off Small Debt or High-Interest Debt?

Many people believe that this is an absurd technique. It teaches you how to pay small debts instead of paying the debts that are costing you more, that is, those that have a higher interest. But the avalanche method aims to pay off debts as soon as possible. If you do, the interest cost will not matter because the debt will not exist for a long time.

Statistics indicate that when you see signs of progress, for example, that you paid a small debt, you get excited. This motivates you to keep paying for what comes next.

If you focus on paying off larger debt with higher interest, you are likely to despair. Not seeing progress, you might end up throwing in the towel. If that happens, we have already lost the battle, because you will not have the motivation to continue on your path to financial freedom and you will resign yourself to living in bankruptcy.

Paying off your debts can take a long time, so be patient. To speed up your process, consider working overtime, or looking for an additional part-time job. Then you can use all the earnings from that job exclusively to pay off the debt. The more radical the life change you make, and the faster you pay your debts, the more successful you will be.

Step # 7 Have Patience and Discipline

Finally, have patience and discipline. Decide once and for all to change your life. It took you a long time to dig the hole you are in. Why wait to get out overnight? Do not give up, and you are going to have good months and others not so good. Focus on the goal of regaining your financial freedom and making financial progress.

All in all, the awesome steps to pay off and destroy your debts forever include:

- Mentality change
- Behavior change
- Spend less than you earn
- Destroy credit cards and stop financing
- Make a budget
- Use the avalanche technique to pay debts
- Have patience and be disciplined

Focus on your goal: achieve financial peace and have the means to change the course of your life. Take care of enjoying your life and not worrying about paying your debts.

4

WIDE RANGE OF WAYS TO SAVE YOUR MONEY

Saving money is the most useful and very rare skill in the modern world. Since we live in an era of financial and political crisis, which has swiftly swept almost the entire civilized world, it does not matter how much you earn today, and tomorrow everything can change. Therefore, you need to learn to limit yourself from unnecessary expenses under any circumstances to take care of your future. Saved money, if they do not save you from the crisis, will simply become a useful investment in the desired acquisition. In this chapter, I'm offering amazing tips to save money and save your budget.

In today's difficult time for most people, it seems that they are saving everything. However, this is a misconception. For the majority, saving is practically giving up everything to have enough money for a salary, enough to pay for a loan, enough for food. Each has its savings. However, it does not become more effective from this. Actually, why is it important to save and how to do it, right?

As one famous traveler said, even a small leak can land even the largest ship aground. A small hole is much more dangerous than a large hole, which can be noticed immediately. Small problems accumulate over the years and solve them already when the collapse is on the verge.

Reasonable, economic people know how to distribute funds correctly. You can save by allocating the same money for other purposes. For example, you can buy 1 kg of sausages (cheap to reduce waste), or you can purchase expensive turkey fillet, but 300 grams, while saving money and not losing in good food. This is a reasonable reallocation of funds.

Is a person saving denying himself almost everything? If so, then this is not a person saving, but a greedy person. Feel the difference? You don't need to count everything to the penny, denying yourself and your family everything you need. Why then live? Why save for quarrels in the family? You need to figure out how to do it right, on what, and why you need to be able to save money. Make a family budget and follow it. Avoid not all, namely unnecessary waste!

Saving Is Good - Saving Is Right. What Cannot Be Denied?

Before you figure out what you need to save on, you need to understand what you cannot deny yourself. You cannot limit yourself to the right food. You can eat less, but quality. Refusing to eat is the wrong method. So you save today on food, and all the money, and even spend more later on treatment.

Also, you do not need to save on vacation. Spending more time, loading yourself up with work without rest and proper sleep, trying to earn all the money in the world is wrong. Why save on vacation? This does not mean spending the last money on a trip and living starving. Live within your means!

Rest – take a barbecue, and a cup of coffee and exciting connections with friends.

Why Is It Important to Save?

A wealthy person is not the one who earns a lot of money, but the one who correctly spends the available income. Even with a minimum wage, you can save even insignificant funds. Why is it important to save? This is a kind of economic culture. Such a subject is not taught at school, nor is it given to students in lectures. And by the way, abroad, "people that are involved in savings" and "rich people" are the same.

A culture of economically sound allocation of funds helps to realize plans. You, as a person, will be independent and successful. No need to save on everything, this is stupid, unpromising, and wrong. But to direct cash flows in the right direction - the correct formation of the foundation for future achievements.

How to Be Economical?

The problem of most of our compatriots is wrong thinking. How to be economical when there is not enough money for anything? To save money, you do not need to wait until you have additional income.

Money has such an unpleasant feature: it is never enough for anyone. The income grows - needs grow.

A few simple rules to help you save money.

#1: Start with A Minimum

No need to put off the entire salary put it under the pillow and admire when everyone around us fell asleep. Start saving with the amount that will be easy for your family. Even if it is a small amount a month, a start will be made! You are just learning to put off.

#2: Postpone Half of the Unplanned Income

Often there are situations when it is possible to earn extra money. These are the "premium" ones that many spend on vacation, shopping, or don't even know what to do with unexpected budget replenishment, attracting unplanned expenses, such as a damaged wheel or the arrival of relatives. Immediately postpone exactly half of the unplanned income, the rest can be used according to the situation.

#3: Count The Trifle

A penny saves, and it is true. How to spend money when the salary is small? Learn to deny yourself the little things for more. A cup of coffee on the street or from a vending machine can be replaced with a package of coffee that still pays off. A walk to the house instead of driving on transport will save money and will serve the body well. Home evenings with friends will help not only to save but also not to depend on the menu and opening hours of the cafe. And there are many such examples in everyone's life.

Trifle in the truest sense of the word. Replace the lunches in the cafe during the lunch break from home, do not throw away discount coupons for purchases in a nearby store, do not be lazy to save on utility bills. Counting your expenses at the end of the month, you will be surprised how much you can save on trifles.

Reasonable distribution of funds - and there are the right savings. Knowing how and where to spend money is already half the success. Knowing where to invest the deferred funds is the secret of entrepreneurship in the future. No need to completely deny yourself the pleasure, just wisely dispose of every penny. Set a goal for which you need to save money. And everything will turn out.

#4: Do Not Order a Main Course

Honestly, the eyes are bigger than the stomach, and we always order too much in the restaurant. We should use this experience to save money. Order only one starter and - if you are still hungry - a dessert. This is usually cheaper than with the main course and still fills us up.

#5: Tickets

Tickets for the cinema or museum are often cheaper online than at the box office. In addition, there are often special offers and coupon codes online. For example, you get two tickets for the price of one.

#6: Voluntary Work at Concerts

Instead of buying an expensive ticket for your favorite band's concert, the next time you could register as a volunteer. Concert organizers are always looking for volunteers to set up the stage or operate the bar. Fortunately, you might even meet your favorite band personally.

#7: Smart Shopping

We all have parts in the closet that we don't wear after one season, and that then acidify in the closet. A second-hand shop is a good place to find custom clothing and even make a little money.

Who said that in saving mode you couldn't spend money at all? It is possible and necessary, but it is worth doing it wisely. Sales, promotions, and stock are the best friends of the thrifty consumer. And the desire to do with things that were in use or rented, if circumstances permit. This does not mean that everything in your home should be second-hand. Just think that you can buy something in almost new condition at a price half that price.

#8: Basics in The Closet

Every woman should have some fashion basics in the closet. With neutral tank tops, jeans and long-sleeved shirts, countless outfits can be created, which in combination with accessories never get boring and are always a good alternative if you have nothing to wear again. Every woman needs these fashion basics in the closet.

#9: Gifts

It doesn't always have to be a particularly expensive gift. Your friends are at least as happy (if not more) about a homemade gift in which you have invested your thoughts and time. Make the greeting card yourself - or how about, for example, homemade beauty products for your best friend? You can easily make a lemon peel for beautiful skin yourself.

#10: Organize Events

Why does it always have to be the bar or the restaurant? Invite your friends to your home or organize a picnic in the city park. So you have all your loved ones around, and no one is forced to spend a lot of money.

Remember, budgeting is the first step towards a reasonable saving of money, which lies in carefully tracking costs. You do not need complex programs and applications; a blank Excel sheet is enough; in which you will write down your expenses line by line for each day. Identical expense items, even small ones like a cup of coffee at lunchtime, enter on one line. At the end of such a row, the amount spent on something once a month (utility bills, snacks at work, movie tickets, spending at the supermarket, etc.) will be reflected, and at the end of each column - the amount spent on a particular day.

#11: Use The Services of Banks

Can't you start saving any small amount? Make an agreement with your payroll bank. He will open another account for you and will automatically transfer to him some agreed amount from each receipt to your payroll account. The main condition is not to withdraw the deferred money unless necessary.

#12: Sell What You Don't Need

Why do you keep things you don't use for a long time? Clothing, books, equipment, everything that is quite suitable for use, but it turned out to be unclaimed, for you can still serve you well. And the proceeds can be a plus to your piggy bank in the bank. When the accumulated reaches a certain amount, you can start investing.

Hence, whether in the supermarket at the checkout or looking at the account statement, many people are familiar with the question of where all the money has gone. And wondering why is there so much month left at the end of the money? It is not always the large purchases that go into your wallet. A lot of small issues add up and ultimately result in surprises.

There are many ways to save some money here and there. The most important thing is the will because where there is a will, there is away. In addition to the options mentioned above, there are many other useful tips. Often, a small question helps, which you consciously ask yourself before the next purchase: Do I need it?

If you change these things in everyday life, you can easily save money. With these tricks, you save money every month, so that at the end of the month some more money is left, you should integrate these simple tricks into your everyday life. And they don't require a significant change.

5

HOW MONEY WORKS?

t somehow happened that we often see people around us, including ourselves, face situations where "there is not enough money" or "there is no money" and other similar things.

At the same time, on the other side, some people always have everything in order with money - they simply exist, because they cannot but be. And if they are not right now, then all that needs to be done is to go and "take" them, meaning to earn. But to earn money is not even in the sense of "hard work to get money," but in the sense of "materializing money," and these are two different things.

And so, carefully examining these two categories of people "who always have no money" and those who always have money, I noticed that those who always have money, for the most part, understand some of the dynamics of money; thus in this chapter, I'll be stating how money works and what you need to do to be part of the categories of people who understand the dynamics surrounding money in its entirety.

I must say right away that I received some of this data by studying some of the disposition of financial experts through their various materials, some from my friends, and some from my personal experience through trial and error.

I will present these things in the form of small notes without arranging them in order of importance. That is, what will be written first does not mean that this is the most important thing. It's better to train yourself to use them in a complex. So let's go!

There Is Money

Reproduce understand this simplicity. There is just money! They are always there! They are everywhere! I always have them! - this is the thought that you simply have in your head. You have them just like you have a body or shoes. Don't worry about losing shoes when you go outside. So with money, do not worry about them - you just have them.

According to financial experts, "money is an idea based on confidence." Well, here is the idea "I have money" - add to it your confidence that you have it and, believe my experience, you will have it. You will have them. But you will have them only when you are one hundred percent sure that you already have them. And please, to hell with your thoughts about the existing reality, the existing reality, a sober approach, and other rubbish telling you that there is no money.

Of course, in one way or another, you will have to erase all the false data that you received in the past, including child-hood [I've extensively discussed this in the previous chapters]. Perhaps someone from your circle told you that "only prostitutes and thieves have money," that "money spoils a person," and so on. With such inferences, you won't earn much.

Look at it differently: the more money, the more good deeds can be made. With the help of money (including) you can achieve a lot, strengthen your personal qualities, get a good education, see the beauty of the world - because all this needs money.

To be rich, you need to love wealth, admire the capable and rich, take a positive example from them, and not envy and even more so hate it.

Once again, here are the working conclusions - "I have money. They simply have nowhere to put. I have a problem with how to spend them. They just got me, everyone goes and goes," and so on. That should be your approach to money when trying to understand the dynamics of money.

Money Smells

Sometimes money smells like fresh air and pleasure, sometimes corpses, broken fates, and sometimes they smell like your sweat and blood, and most often it is the smell of slave labor. You decide what your money will smell like. But from experience I can say the following: sometimes it happens that you were taught and finally taught to make money and to make money very well, but this money is heartily received from a product sold through kickbacks, or it was obtained by deceiving the state, or, do not let god, from drug sales and so on. They are just with a shower. And you have become a pro in making "money with a dink." You know all about it. You are a master at this, and, of course, you have a lot of excuses for why this is normal. Well ... in this case, the transition from money with a sickening smell to money, smelling mountain air, saved lives or real, genuine pleasure, will be difficult. The path will be very difficult. And yet it is worth it to have money smelling of fresh, ringing air, and not of fresh graves.

Earn Money Before You Need It

What simplicity. And how difficult it is to understand and even more so to do. And yet - make money before you need it.

Good, let's look in more detail, what does this phrase mean?

Firstly, this means - earn more than you need to meet all your needs and the needs of your family (by the way, this applies to the company). Of course, you can say that the needs of any person are unlimited, and when he has an apartment, he wants his own house. When he has a house, he wants a villa. When there is a villa, he wants another villa, plus an airplane, plus a yacht, plus, and so on. Well, great game - and earn more than you need. On the other hand, no one forbids you to establish reasonable boundaries of needs, but remember that this is a trap. It will be much better if you periodically pick up and pick up your bar of "reasonable" needs, as stated in the chapter on "how to reduce and control wants."

Secondly, the phrase means "prudent financial planning of upcoming expenses." Look ahead, figure out what you will need the money in the coming year. Sit down and WRITE (hear, sit down and write down) all your spending plans for the coming year. And please do not rely on available income. I'll explain now that a person sits on a salary that is barely enough for food and some clothes.

Of course, focusing on his current income, you cannot write "buy an apartment," but, without completely breaking away from reality, you can still write something close to buying an apartment. You may still want to buy it. You can still go and choose it, and then start to create your life for new tasks and goals. And then we will make money before we need to spend it on a new apartment? Who said, what is impossible? You? So change your conclusions.

Another example of the second definition: You are going to go abroad for some training. This training will require you a lot of expenses, suppose one hundred thousand dollars. Options: to borrow and go now and get all the stunning victories and successes from studying now or postpone the trip to a later date and first earn money before you go there before you need them. The answer is clear - make money and then go. This is the rational financial planning of future expenses.

This explains, "make money before you need it." So everything is simple.

Money Is Easier to Earn Than to Borrow

I went through this. As it once seemed to me, well, now there are problems, creditors do not just put pressure, they threaten, they do not let me sleep at night, I hid my family, cops refuse to help, bandits are not on your side, well, now I will borrow, and all will be well. It Will not be. You will have to, if of course, you want to live a normal life, stop this vicious cycle of "interception in debt." You will have to go through this without hiding or avoiding - to meet with creditors, bandits, with the devil himself bald and settle all of them, make them all wait.

And roll up your sleeves yourself and earn. Yes, it happens that you encounter a steam rink called a bank, where you have mortgaged property, and its loss will exceed many times the amount of your debt. Well, in this situation, it would be wiser to borrow, close the problem, but solve for yourself, what was the last time you borrowed. Solve it for real.

Decide that even if you and your family have to go hungry, you will no longer borrow money. Nowadays, it is difficult to die of hunger. They just won't give. And, accordingly, this rule will not give you a single chance to retreat. It will be difficult for you. You will have a break, you will be flattened and "sausage" - well, nothing. Weaning from this drug "living on credit" is always accompanied by withdrawal. Nobody was dying from this withdrawal, but the ability to have money has always increased.

Categorically Do Not Borrow Money for A Living or for "Eating at A Company"

Given the above, let us look at this from a slightly different point of view. When you take money not for creating new money, but for life, you. There are a lot of terrible things happening: you can begin to feel as if you are a little inferior; you sign your inability to take care of yourself on your own; you humiliate yourself; you are not all right with your ethics; you begin to introvert and collapse your space and so forth.

And when you, the company you are heading, take a loan, either for wages, for utility bills, or rent, the same thing will happen to you and your employees as described above in this section. Only everything will be worse - you will be pressured by responsibility, you will physically feel this pressure, you will begin to sleep poorly, many will start to drink little by little.

At home you will become uncomfortable, you will begin to growl at your wife, look for the guilty, someone strikes in search of outlet and peace on the side with his mistress. Yes, my friend - here, whether you like it or not, many different "miracles" will occur. Of course, if without the extremes described by me, then there is no problem intercepting money in debt for the company to close temporary cash gaps.

But, in any case, even this trifle will, to one degree or another, mean that you didn't get from production employees, you have not perfect financial planning, and maybe problems in sales, PR or a bad product. Anything, there may be many reasons, but among them, there is one main thing - you, as a manager, can't cope with their duties.

And either you can switch the toggle switch in your head in the right direction and make things go right, or you urgently need to be replaced by someone who can correct the situation. There are no other solutions.

If You Borrow Money, Borrow It for Something That Belongs to You and with Which You Are Ready to Part Easily

This is so simple. And it's not even that you have to give something as a guarantee; it's just that you have to fulfill your obligations unless, of course, you want to get the stigma of an optional comrade who cannot be trusted.

Trust is worth more than the thing that you could sell to fulfill your obligations. Restoring trust is always more expensive than temporarily losing a particular thing that you have to sell to repay the debt on time. And this willingness to sacrifice something disciplines and makes you move. I do not want to part with things - move. But always remember - the brand of a talker will cost you many times more.

And the question here is not even what people will think about you, people today thought, and tomorrow they forgot, there are things worse than the lost reputation of a reliable person. The question here is that no matter how you reassure yourself, no matter how you justify yourself, you will be breaking, crushing, executing because there is no executioner next to you stronger than yourself. So this situation works like the law of universal gravitation, and it cannot be repealed.

Money Can Only Be Borrowed to Create New Money

Money is energy. If you borrow energy to create new energy and take them under something that you can easily part with, then go ahead. We sit down and consider: we take a loan of 10 million at 20 percent per annum. Monthly turnover rate. In a year, the money will be wrapped up 12 times. On each turnover, we earn 20 percent.

Moreover, after fulfillment of all-all obligations related to the circulation of money (salaries, taxes, transportation, kickbacks, overhead, communal services, interest to the bank, repayment of the loan body, and many more), 2 percent of the earned 20 percent remains. For 12 months, this is 24 percent of 10 million. Well - if all of this is true and all this is doable, then, of course, in this case, it is beneficial to take out a loan because you will make money on it.

Or you are currently renting an apartment and pay 30 thousand a month for it. And if you buy an apartment on a mortgage, you will pay the bank 35 thousand a month, but you will live in your "own" (in quotation marks) apartment. And even though it will cost you at least twice as much, it is still a profitable deal with a bank, if there is no way to buy it in advance.

You Can Create Energy in The Form of Money from Nothing

It's as simple as I wrote. And until you believe this, you will not have enough money. I do not know how to explain and convey this. But look at those businessmen who started from scratch. Not for those who "grabbed" by deceit and flattery the pipe at collateral auctions (also that scheme), but for those guys who did everything from scratch.

Many of them made billions, starting from scratch and not even taking money to promote. But even when they borrowed money for promotion, they returned it, and still, it turns out that they started from scratch. There is a certain "X" quality that they possess, and it is thanks to this quality that investors, banks, and friends have trusted them.

Maybe it will be such a commonplace as:
- Worked physically at a construction site - bought a computer;
- Using a computer, conducted market research on... "People's needs for happiness";
- While continuing to work at a construction site, I found out that people consider "happiness" and how much they are willing to pay for creating this happiness;
- Developed the project of "creating happiness," gave advertising and began to earn money on "happiness";
- Hired people who, under your leadership, will sell a lot of "happiness."

And so on. The main thing is that your idea will conquer the world and people would pay you millions for it. Here you have money from nothing.

The simplicity here lies in the fact that the first is always the idea, checking demand, it is possible to create demand (a bright example of creating demand for new products is Apple). Then money will certainly appear underneath all this. Ideas give rise to money. Great ideas generate a lot of money. The idea is always primary. Hence, you can create energy in the form of money from nothing.

The Amount of Money That You Will Have Will Be Equal to The Amount of What You Want to Spend It On

And it doesn't matter if there is money now. It doesn't matter that all the circumstances are against you. It doesn't matter that right now, there are no ideas, no thoughts, and indeed real reality tells you that all this is impossible. Formulate as accurately as possible what you want to spend them on. Describe it.

Go to the store and select this. Hang a picture of it on the wall. Talk to each family member. Make every family member want to buy it too and just start working on this goal, not paying attention to existing barriers, existing reality.

The existing reality "allows" you to make ends meet in half with grief. Well, to hell with such a reality. You now have new big goals - here and create a new reality for new goals. Of course, this may require courage from you, and you may have to change your life habits completely, change your sphere of activity, sit down to learn at night, you will have to go through persuading your loved ones not to risk it and so on.

Well, you have to choose - impoverished stability or drive along with sleepless nights for the next few years with the opportunity to be proud of yourself and ensure a comfortable old age. With the ability to take care of his wife and children, or to live "like all normal people."

For me, it's better to be not normal and rich than normal, requiring your wife to plow because "I am not a slave to provide you with every- thing here."

I Wrote About This Above, But I Want to Highlight This Separately for Clarity

Money borrowed for personal consumption is slamming your space. Debts kill your abilities. Debts make you small and miserable. Having borrowed money for personal consumption, even if it is something sacred, such as future freedom, you are destroying your abilities, and the stronger you become on the path to freedom, the more you will bury yourself and trap you. Sad, Of course, there are, as it seems, exceptions to this rule. But this is the apparent exception. This "exception," which did not bury itself, getting freedom in debt, would be ten times stronger if it made money before it was needed.

Do Not Lend Money for Personal Consumption

You thus deprive a person of power and do him a disservice. If you want to help him, there are thousands of ways to help without lending money. In extreme cases, give him money as a charity (war, refugees - anything can happen). Or, if this is your sister, brother, just help as much as possible, without humiliating them with your money and encouraging them to move.

But there is another trap. Very often, when you give a person a loan for his personal needs, you earn a lot of problems for your hard-earned money. As a rule, people who borrow for personal needs either repay the debt inappropriately or try not to repay it at all.

Sometimes it comes to the point of absurdity. The debtor can tell you: "well, for you, it's a penny, you don't be able to live without this money," and he begins to carry on all nonsense, letting you know that you are a bad person. You made it so that now he hated you, you lost a friend, and if the amount of debt is large, then you are now in danger because the law "no man - no problem" has not been canceled.

And all this is only because you once stepped on your throat, justified, "Which can be difficult for you and you may have to borrow" and gave him the same money for personal consumption. If you are lending money for personal consumption to another person, keep in mind the following:

- You must be prepared for default on debt. You must be prepared to lose this money.
- Always draw up such things in writing, but rather draw them up in accordance with all the legal subtleties. And do not care what you give to a friend or brother and that he will think about you. He will think that you are a serious guy, it's better not to joke with you.
- And perfect - apply for a deposit in the amount of your loan. And take something from this guy as a guarantee that you can easily sell for half the price and fully cover the amount of the loan given to him. And arrange everything so that this thing passed into your ownership at one minute of the first night after the expiration of the date of repayment of the debt.
- And if you don't want to do all this, don't want to have possible hemorrhoids, don't want to spoil your relationship, then don't give money for personal consumption.

"And, of course, learn to say NO." And whatever your sweet "YES," the unpleasant "NO" will save your nervous system and make your life and the life of the asker happier.

Give Back Something Valuable, Something That You Are Ready To Pay For, And Only Then Get The Money

But in any case, when you receive money, always provide something more valuable than these worthless pieces of paper. "They owe me" because I am, or because I go to work - this is the most reliable way to live my whole life from paycheck to paycheck with a periodic loss of work. And this is always anger at the authorities, grunts, excuses, and life in a fog, never coming true hopes.

And even more so, this situation applies to companies, nations, and states. Respect based on a nuclear bomb is negligible compared to respect based on a prosperous economy, happy and free citizens.

Big Money Is Not Earned at Work

Big money is earned when creating work for others. All around you are full of people willing to work for a paycheck. So give them a paid job and have a lot of money. You will make pay recipients happy by giving them jobs, creating jobs, and will have tons of money.

If You Direct All Your Attention, All Your Energy to Borrow, You Will Have Many Debts

And if you direct your energy and attention to creating money by providing society with something valuable, you will have a lot of money and a lot of honor and respect. You always get what you reward for a long time with your energy and your attention.

Do Not Connect Your Life with Whiners and Beggars

Failure to have money is the same infection, like the flu. You don't have time to blink an eye, as you will catch the disease, "I can't have anything."

Always Support Those Who Are Stronger, More Capable, Smarter and Richer Than You

Help them. Support them. Strengthen them, and you will become stronger and richer. Saving the wretched, it can be honorable, but in this case, be aware that you too will sooner or later become wretched, and then there will be someone who will already support your squalor.

Do Not Spend Honestly Earned Money in One Mug - Everything Will, Burst and There Will, Be Nowhere to Add Money

Engage in charity, save society at your own expense. Do not wait for the government to save you. What is surprising here is that the more you do. Sincerely, you will spend money on saving society, the more you will have it. Only help sincerely, from the heart. And help those projects that are aimed at creating and eliminating the vices of society, such as drug addiction, illiteracy, crime, and so on. And, of course, help the elderly and orphans. Help artists at least that do not steal their copyrights, buying counterfeit works. Try it. Just try to give away the first thousand. Further, it will be easier.

Money Goes to The One Who Knows How to Attract Attention

Once my acquaintance, a well-known accountant in England, rejoicing, showed me an article from BBC where he, as a professional, was razed to the ground. I asked him: "What are you happy about? This is a devastating article." He answered me: "You don't understand anything. They made me a great advertisement. Now everyone knows me.

"They call me and say, well, since you already have a sad experience, and such a newspaper wrote about you, probably you have learned a lot, and now we want to make an order for you."

Of course, it is better to attract positive attention to yourself and your products, goods, services. But always remember that negative attention is better than its complete absence.

Don't Promise

Never promise money to anyone if you haven't earned it yet, or if you don't have 100% sources of their income and you cannot accurately name all sources of money, dates, approximate amounts, and most importantly, for what exactly are you get them and what are the guarantees of their receipt.

Just the hope of receiving, just a great thought about your abilities to have money and so on - not bad, but it does not work. What I wrote works. It always works, everywhere, on all the planets of this universe. Usually, having promised money, not having clear, reliable sources of their receipt, but having only hope, a person automatically begins to attract failures. And if he had not promised, then perhaps his hopes would have come true, but here - as luck would have it, everything is against him.

Is Not Your Money

The money from your company (if you are the owner of this company) is not your money. Yours are the only constituent, and the rest of the money belongs to the company and is at the disposal of your employees. This is the energy with which your employees create even more money for you. And if you start your paw in the money of the company, you will betray employees, lose their trust, and you will no longer have money.

Money Has Its Purpose

If you put aside money to buy an office or a necklace for your wife - that's all; you put a stamp on them. You plunged them into the abyss of water. You buried them a hundred kilometers underground. Forget about them. And no matter how difficult it may be, whatever the irresistible desire to get into a small pillow and take money from there for some holy work or, well, I'll take it to (think of a reason for yourself) - do not do this.

Money is always easier to make than to take from hidden corners. As soon as you take the money that bears the stigma of a "new office" and spend it on holy, you will lose to the same extent. Each penny has a purpose. Save to the car - save to the car and don't touch them until you go to the salon to get the car.

You, observing this, may encounter a bunch of reasons why you need to forget about your dream and immediately spend money on something more "valuable." Advice - do not get fooled. And if what you are offered is more valuable, then make money on it without touching the money set aside for your dream - a new car or a necklace for your wife. Money has its purpose.

Create A Cash Reserve

Create a cash reserve (airbag) in case of problems and make it so that you never have to use this airbag. But you will notice, having a reserve, it will be easier to operate with money, which means that you will have more money.

Prioritizing The Spending of Earned Money

Of course, as it seems, first of all, you need to invest in your abilities or in what will bring you new money. But this is only an apparent thing, and it works poorly.

First of all, spend money on something material for yourself and your loved ones. For something very desirable for yourself - create a desire to spend money on yourself.

Encourage yourself, as a source of income, with something valuable and material - an expensive villa, an expensive car, and so on. Then do not forget to spend a lot of money on your investment object, on your pride, your love - on your wife, children, mother ... and only then invest in your abilities and invest. This is not absolute. These things can and should be done in parallel.

Take Risk

Remember, the one who does not take risks, he works for a paycheck. So take risks, but always, when you take risks, be prepared to be left without pants. You see if you plan to win - fine. Direct all your forces to victory. But before you start, calculate and look at what will happen if you lose. And if you are ready to lose - then forward to victory. If you are not ready to lose - do not meddle because most likely, you will lose.

Your Income

Your income is directly proportional to your ability to control money positively. Money loves accounting and control. If your financial director is not able, from memory, to tell you the exact numbers how much your company earned last month, last quarter, last week - he is not able to control the money, and I do not think that he is a good financial director.

A productive person, able to have and control money, always knows how much he and his company have earned, how much and where they spent, and he always has this data at hand. Money loves control. No control - no money. Bad control - bad with money. Good control means satiety, creditworthiness, a bright future.

Pay Only for A 100% Product

Pay only for a 100% product, a 100% quality result you need. Never pay for work done halfway. And even for work done at 99%, do not pay either. Be irreconcilable in this. Pay Only for Valuable End Product

Do Not Spend Money Off Wheels

Do not spend your money on the wheels. Always plan your income and expenses. Then, when the money is earned, sit down and plan the distribution of this money. To hell with those who suffer and ask. To hell with urgency, all to hell. This is your money. Sit and plan where you will take them and only then spend them. Never spend money outside the plan (except in emergency cases such as getting sick)

Never Count On the State

The goal of any state on the planet is to make you beggar, make you dependent on handouts and quirks of the authorities, to make you an obedient voter through promises and petty handouts in the form of social benefits. So you should not count on a good ruler - he is kind only on TV and exactly as much as it is required to cause your delight.

You Can Buy Everything Except Conscience

You can buy everything except your conscience, honor, love, support of your relatives and friends. Treasure your honor, conscience, and those with whom you are bound by bonds of love and friendship. Otherwise, you will not have money, or they will stink and stink.

Crumbs Are Earned Upon Receipt of a Paycheck

This is a salary job in the absence of a clearly expressed product. This is a voluntary burning of life in the status of a vegetable.

Money for life and, possibly, for some interests in life are earned at work when you receive wages for something valuable that you do for the company. There is already a risk of receiving part or all of the money in the form of interest, bonuses, bonuses, and other things tied to the result.

Money that allows you to live a fairly full life is earned when responsibility is added to the previous one, and you become the head of the department head to the director of the company.

Further, it would be possible to derive several more levels, and you could come up with some kind of name, but the last level, where you earn money that is enough for "Everything," is the level of the Game. This is the level when you are not working, and you are playing. Well, remember how you played a game in your childhood! Remember how this game captures you! Remember that drive, then the state of XYXY. Now imagine that in the same way, playing and playing, you can materialize money.

Don't Waste Your Life

Do not waste your life on social networks, idle chatter, stupid people, and other useless things - they will not bring you any money or happiness.

Life, of course, cannot be measured in money. Happiness cannot be measured in money either, and you cannot buy it for any money. But it so happened that it is better to have money in search of happiness than to build your happiness in poverty.

Money Goes to Someone Who Is Ready

Money goes to someone ready to be the cause and takes responsibility for all the consequences associated with making money.

The rich are sure - "I am the creator of my life," the poor know for sure - "nothing depends on me." The poor feel like a victim of circumstances, and all that they are rich in is accusations, excuses, complaints.

Learn from The Rich

The rich know how to plow," tearing off fingers in the blood, "learn from their own and others' mistakes, just learn, absorbing all the successful experience, and each of them is sure that he is the creator of his happiness."

It's not enough to sit and meditate about the fact that "Money is coming to me like a river," you also need to work. And please, get the idea out of your head that if a person is rich, then he is a swindler, and everything goes to him easily and fun. The vast majority of businessmen are talented people who achieve success "with their sweat and blood."

Your Income Is Directly Proportional to Your Value

And, of course, this banality (as it would seem): Our income is directly proportional to our value - how many people we can help.

How many people help our product (product or service)? How much we solve or satisfy the needs of the maximum number of people. How widely do we reach those who can pay, and so forth?

Hence, no matter how wild it may sound, but to begin with, tell yourself that you are the best, and then become one. I did not pretend and do not pretend that I have described all you need to know about how money works. But perhaps my insight will help you earn more and get, thanks to this, a little more financial freedom.

6

EFFECTS OF POOR MONEY MANAGEMENT

How do you know if you are managing your finances well or badly? If you earn between $1,500 and $2,500 per month (or between $3,000 and $5,000 for a couple without children), you are part of the middle class.

You pay a lot of taxes without being helped by the redistribution because you "earn too much" to receive aid. Finally, "you earn too much," it quickly says…

Daily, you do not have the impression of living comfortably. And that is the problem. Once the accommodation (rent or loan repayment) and the constrained charges paid, you try to enjoy life, but also to protect yourself from hard times, to prepare the studies of the children, to save for the retirement.

But is it possible to balance all of this? Is it normal to struggle despite a good salary? After all, it's a "crisis" all the time, isn't it? It is natural to doubt: money is taboo. It is impossible to know whether the bank overdraft is part of a "normal" financial life or whether it is hiding something else.

And it is not with your colleagues that you can discuss it ... or very superficially. Everyone only shows their successes... As for your banker, he is judge and jury.

As a person with experiences from different financial coaches and trainers in budget management, they have helped hundreds of people get out of the overdraft, save, and reorganize their finances to reach ambitious goals. Suffice to say that they have seen very different situations.

Today, from this experience, I'll share with you 11 symptoms of financial mismanagement, along with advice that will help you progress.

11 signs that something is wrong with your bank account management

1. You Are Overdrawn

And there you are, you're in the red! This means that your expenses are greater than your resources and that the bank has lent you the difference. Because the overdraft is indeed a credit.

2. You Juggle Between Multiple Accounts

The joint account, personal account, account with the bank which granted the loan, account opened in an online bank in exchange for a premium. Do you need as many bank accounts?

The multiplication of accounts leads to confusion and errors. It can also cause you to imagine wrong solutions when needed money (No, fill the overdraft of an account with an overdraft of another is not a good idea).

3. You Use Revolving Credit

It is easy, and advertising encourages you to do so: revolving credit is within everyone's reach. But it is expensive and keeps you under the illusion that you have more money than you have. Worse: it encourages you to postpone real management efforts.

Remain very vigilant in the face of revolving credit proposals and the (very badly named) "money reserves." The revolving credit is harmful to the borrower. It opens the door to further problems. If you fell into this trap, repay it a priority.

4. You Have Late Payments

You refuse credits but take advantage of payment facilities as soon as possible. You know all the optimizations: payments in three installments at no cost, co-ownership charges that may drag on, such a supplier that can be delayed, sports associations asking on what date they can cash the check.

But you have to face the facts: by delaying payments, you create debts. You are blowing today, but a surprise discovery may fall on you soon. Instead, try to create provision savings for your projects, your life will be much more peaceful.

5. You Are Subject to The Unexpected

In itself, the unexpected is not a sign of mismanagement: everyone can be subject to it. It is what happens after that makes the difference: managing your money well is being able to minimize the consequences of the vagaries of life thanks to precautionary savings, which will play the role of a shock absorber. No longer suffer, follow my guide in this book on precautionary savings to be able to take hardships without being in trouble.

6. You're Not Saving

You can't save money. You try, but you end up recovering the money quickly, sometimes in the weeks that follow.
However, without savings, you stagnate (in the best of cases) and risk capsizing (in the worst of cases).

To save sustainably, set yourself goals, be clear about your desires and motivations, adopt good savings habits, and build a long-term heritage.

7. You Are Ashamed

Having an overdraft or card blocking is already humiliating. But it is even more so when your professional life is successful: you earn a good living, you have a position of responsibility and are unable to manage your account?

Regain confidence in yourself. The world of banking products is deliberately opaque. Also, financial management is very dependent on family learning patterns. You are prob- ably more a victim than a culprit.

8. You Feel Unable to Prepare for The Future

Everything escapes you. You are a puppet for the banks. They tell you what you have the right to do and what day to do it. You live day by day, crossing your fingers so that tomorrow brings no misfortune.
Put money back where it belongs: it should serve you, not the other way around. It must allow you to project yourself into the future, and for this, a budget is essential.

9. Your Bank Account Is Stressing You Out

Reading this title already stresses you out. Two possible attitudes: either you consult your bank balance several times a day (sorry but no, you will not be able to make your balance go up by hypnosis), or you avoid at all costs looking at it (because what remains hidden can't reach you, of course…).

Your finances should not put you in this state. I devoted a chapter on "How Money Works" to help you understand the dynamics of your finances and to easily avert financial distress and the long road to get out of it.

10. You Lead a Double Life

You seem to be hiding a terrible secret. On the front, every- thing is fine. Behind it is chaos. And when money is raised within the couple, it always ends badly. You sometimes practice financial infidelity: you hide expenses from your spouse and even from yourself, thanks to selective memory. You should talk about it, you know, but talking about money is often difficult. Each couple must find a personal organization for the management of their finances.

11. You Are Waiting for A Miracle

Do you dream of a magic wand that erases your debts and makes you rich? Having goals in life is good, but miracles do not exist. The solutions must come from yourself. However, "taking charge" does not necessarily mean "staying alone."

Have you recognized yourself in these symptoms of flawed management?

If you've recognized yourself in one, two, or ten of these symptoms, you might think you need more money. But money is not everything: it is useless if you keep bad habits. You don't need a patch. You need solid foundations that will permanently improve your situation and avoid future difficulties. All the solutions in this book go in this direction. Admittedly, confronting the problems in front can be emotionally difficult. This certainly requires persistence, courage, humility, and possibly to challenge your vision of money. But it is indeed necessary to move forward.

7

THE ROAD TO SUCCESS

On your road to success, one of the essential things is your habits to achieve your goals. The differences often come from daily habits, and for 40% of unconscious actions that we carry out in a day, which means that for almost half of the time, we live on automatic pilot. According to studies done in the USA, the gap between the habits of the rich and those of the poor is staggering, especially since some are obvious, others more surprising.

Habits are our second nature.

They make us act and think stereotypically. And to do so again and again, despite the unsatisfactory results obtained. Thus, the habit of buying things by installments or credit deprives us of the opportunity to manage our income fully.

The actions that we perform daily or in a specific situation, that is, our habits, depending on the way of thinking. By changing your perceptions of the world, in particular, ideas about wealth and rich people, you can earn more.

People who inherit or win large sums in the lottery do not often become millionaires. Because they don't know how to handle money. Scientists say that poor people have a psychological ban on wealth. Since there is a stereotype in our society that it is impossible to become a millionaire honestly.

Researcher Thomas Corley was trying to understand the difference between the behavior and habits of a person earning millions of dollars from people whose annual income was below $150 thousand. He found that most millionaires have the same habits and lifestyles. He gives the figures that were obtained from a survey of 233 people with high annual incomes and 128 whose incomes were low.

44% of wealthy people wake up at least three hours before work. Only about 3% of the poor do this. 88% of millionaires read daily, giving it half an hour. Although among the poor, 26% said they like to read, only 2% do it every day.

Among the habits of wealthy people, Corley notes that 67% write down their goals. As the survey showed, the rich do not watch TV and reality shows but prefer to play sports and lead a healthy lifestyle.

Let's take a closer look at what habits unite people who have managed to earn millions of dollars.

1. Believe in Your Free Will and Dream

Daily habits are essential to financial success. The rich man is convinced that its action impacted his life, that a bad habit creates prejudice and good creating opportunities, opportunities to act, and take this opportunity. The rich man firmly believes that he is lucky when the poor man considers himself lucky; more than luck, one believes in him. This dream is possible for him, he is convinced that life offers him unlimited potential, and he is ready to invest the time necessary to achieve this dream wealth.

The poor most often believe that their fate is linked to genetics, their family tree of the poor, and, therefore, that they are not responsible for their financial situation. The rich, who most of the time have not always been rich, are aware of their power to make a difference.

2. Exploit, Maintain, Help Relationships, And Love

For him instinctively, others are essential to his success, and also the colossal efforts he must provide; he knows how to call them regularly to congratulate them, encourage them or help them or just greet them and hear from them. It is adding fuel to the wheels of success. He enjoys meeting new people, values his contacts, and arouses maximum sympathy. He is convinced that loved and appreciated will increase his financial success.

Also, the willingness to share is essential. Most wealthy people are distinguished by their generosity. They participate in charity work, sponsor social and scientific programs, and become philanthropists. They are ready to help other people, but only if they want it. Do not treat money as a goal, and it is just a means to achieve it.

Thus, communicate with people, make contacts. Other people pay us money. A wide circle of friends will help you quickly find investors or potential buyers.

Love is the religion of any millionaire. Love - must become a habit. With it, you can build the future and protect the rear. Love for what you do, family, relatives, friends, and colleagues will help you overcome all the difficulties on the way to the top. Love is fuel for our main muscles. If you have an opinion about the spread of love around the world, then you will become successful.

But never love money the most. A smooth transition from ambition and desire to make the world a better place to greed is a slippery slope. Focusing on money can help you become richer, but that does not mean that you will feel happiness.

According to statistics, almost 70% of winners in large lotteries are fatal after 7 years. Money, and especially easy money, spoils people and destroys them. The key to true success is that you love regardless of them.

"It's sad to see when a person has studied economics but never studied happiness," said entrepreneur Jim Rohn. According to a study in Thomas Corley's book, Rich Habits, 86% of people who loved their jobs had a net worth of about $ 3.6 million.

3. Live Within Your Means and Save Money

The rich a priori knows how to earn a lot of money but above all to save money and accumulate wealth. Many poor people are rich people who did not know how to keep their money, instead of applying the 50%/30%/20% rule. 50% for the "needs," 30% for "wants," and 20% for "savings." The rich avoid spending too much, while those who struggle generally have a lifestyle beyond their means and go into debt.

Most people increase their expenses in proportion to the increase in income. So, if you raised your salary, then again, it all goes to the acquisition. Rich people do not try to spend money right away, and they save it before they are successfully invested. One must learn to live on a certain amount, and when received, moreover, create savings for passive income. You need to plan your expenses and not make impulsive purchases correctly. The mentioned Warren Buffett, who occupies the third place in the Forbes list, lives in a house that he bought back in 1957 for a little more than $30 thousand.

4. Use Your Creativity More Than Your Intelligence

Creativity is essential to financial success; the wealthy often show inventiveness and imagination; for the poor to become rich, it is necessary to be intellectually gifted, or wealth most often arises accidentally. The poor impose self-limiting beliefs and often think that they cannot become rich.

5. Enjoy Working and Do a Lot

He likes, if not adores, his work. It is no coincidence that he works more than 50 hours per week, and the fact of loving what he does potentiates his creativity, which turns into monetary value. The poor work to eat and get bored without adding value to what they do and, therefore, without being able to get rich.

Those who are struggling are paralyzed by the habit of limiting their work to their job description. He never gives more, and his salary stagnates from year to year if he keeps his job. The wealthy make themselves indispensable in the eyes of their employer or their clients, work hard to achieve a collective goal from which they ultimately gain enrichment.

6. Enjoy Good Health and Take Risks

Good health is essential for financial success; it is obvious, no one can earn money in a hospital bed; for everyone, less illness means less absence and more productivity.

The rich see opportunities in everything which he'd take the risk for. For a person going to financial independence, glass is not half empty, but one in which you can add water. He does not focus on problems and why this happened but quickly searches for ways to solve or eliminate them.

The rich person is rarely rich on the first try, he has often suffered failures and has hardened himself by taking hits, he is not afraid of failure and risks it, this is how often he can grasp the right opportunity. The poor often find their failures very bad, keeping scars that hurt them and prevent them from renewing their initiatives.

7. Read A Lot and Avoid the Internet

Read yes but not just anything, information that increases your knowledge of your company, your sector, your profession or your career, which makes you more efficient and more interesting for your colleagues, your customers. The rich make good use of their reading time on their journey, devour books for personal development, biographies of successful leaders, and keep themselves informed of current events. He reads because he wants to improve, to increase his knowledge, to identify opportunities better.

The poor often read little, and when he does, it is rare for his self-improvement, but entertainment in front of a TV, time- consuming and costly bad habit.

You need to improve gaining to acquire new knowledge and applying innovative technologies, and you can create a product that will bring millions. Read books on management, improve knowledge in your industry, keep abreast of events - this will set you apart from competitors. Eighty- five- year- old Warren Buffett, whose fortune is more than 60 billion dollars, calls the best investment in life to read the book "Intelligent Investor" B. Graham.

The majority of the rich hardly watch it on TV, they surf the Internet for professional reasons, preferring to use their free time in personal development, voluntary actions, the pursuit of a noble goal, or the practice of a sport or a hobby.

Thus, surround yourself with rich purposeful people. If your environment does not believe that a person without connections and a lot of capital can get rich, then you will lose this faith and give up. Having a real example, you will strive to achieve the same success. If there is no authority nearby, read the biographies of billionaires, find out how they achieved wealth.

8. Control and Overcome Your Emotions

Not every emotion is good to be expressed. When you say everything that goes on in your mind, you often risk hurting yourself. Easy and uncontrolled speech is often noticed in those who are fighting financially.

The rich filter his emotions and control them; he knows how to wait for the calm of his mood to speak and to consider a situation objectively. In particular, it overcomes the fear of changing, of making mistakes, of taking risks or of failing.

9. Avoid Procrastination and Set Goals

You cannot control the outcome of a wish, but that of a goal. Each year, the majority of the wealthy pursue at least one major goal. It is to fight against procrastination, which harms the quality of the action. Everyone has their tips, such as creating to-do lists every day or making themselves "do it now."

Also, set global goals. If the task is to earn a certain amount, then you will receive it. To begin, set a goal to earn 5 thou- sand dollars. You can do more, but no less. And go to your goal in small daily steps. The right goals are those that are realistic to fulfill and depend only on you and not on the weather, other people, or fortune.

Hence, do not put off until later. Once you have made your decision, take action. Do not drag out, someone can realize your idea, and you will be left with nothing. Do not wait for a "convenient" moment; you can miss your chance. Have read useful information - start using it. If you act under the motto of Scarlett, "Think about it tomorrow," you will never get rich.

Make an action plan for the day, week, month, year. You need to know what you have to do today to achieve your great goal. In this regard, both day off and vacation should be spelled out, but there should be no blank pages.

The rich person acts instead of putting off until tomorrow, and he knows how to refrain from speaking to listen; in doing so, he learns a lot, understands others better, and can act opportunely. Despite the setbacks, it often persists when the poor stop pursuing their goal and stop.

10. Do Not Stop

You don't have to stop on your road to success. The rich keep on striving no matter the challenges; hence, go to your goal no matter what. Even if it seems that there is no way out, look at the problem from a different angle. It may be worth taking a step back, but do not betray the dream.

Most of today's millionaires have been defeated more than once; what they did was not profitable. But none of them gave up and found the right path. Treat failure as an invaluable experience. Three students came up with a mobile service for exchanging self-destructing messages in 10 seconds. The project was unsuccessful, and one of the developers, quarreling with friends, abandoned it. The application was finalized, and today Evan Spiegel and Bobby Murphy have a fortune of 2.1 billion and 1.8 billion, respectively.

11. Think Outside the Box

The rich always find the solution to most things around him by thinking outside the box. So to be in this category on your road to success, you need to learn to think outside the box. Income can bring completely unexpected things. Paul Brown, the creator of the bottle, which is placed on the lid, was able to sell the business and design rights for $14 million. The inventor of the Rainbow children's bright toy earned about $250 million on it. The idea came when he saw how a metal spring fell and began to "step over" the floor. The creator of stickers, his idea helped to earn more than a billion dollars.

12. Appreciate Your Time

You need to appreciate your time. Rich people do not consider how much they earn per month or year, but how much they earn per hour. Review your day and consider what actions do not benefit your health, business, or family. Exclude watching useless films, secular correspondence on social networks, empty conversations on the phone, and you will find temporary resources for self-education, planning, and for a good rest.

13. Say, "NO."

To be able to say no is a useful quality in life. When you gain courage and utter this word in response to sentences that do not suit you, you thereby save your own time, money, and maybe even nerves.

You should be able to refuse the next party with your friends if you do not want to go to it. Do not be afraid of resentment, and true friends will be obliged to support you in your choice. By doing this, you will get the right time to develop yourself. Use it well: study, sign up for courses, learn new things, get enough sleep, do work that will help you advance your career.

Financially independent people can say no. Oddly enough, but this word changes the way of life and frees you from everything wasteful unless, of course, you pronounce it in the "right places."

14. Invest

The habits of the rich naturally extend to relationships with money. If you suddenly managed to earn a ton of money - this is just great! But the lack of financial literacy, under- standing of reasonable cost savings, and investing can deprive you of a solid income in a few days or months. Abandoned squandering and lack of knowledge on how to manage money leads to disaster

Successful and wealthy people study the market and its tools, select profitable and reliable assets in which they invest their money. Also, they regularly save part of the income for the emergency fund and the savings fund, and only then they think about the necessary expenses and purchases.

15. Follow Your Passion

Steve Jobs said that everyone should find a favorite pastime. The only way to become rich and be happy is to immerse yourself in your favorite business. Not one person will succeed in an activity that he does not like.

86% of the rich love what they earn for a living. When you like what you do, you devote more time to it. This allows you to hone your skills more productively. More reading time to earn all about your calling. More time in building relation- ships with other success-oriented people in your industry. More time committed to improving yourself makes you more valuable and rich.

16.   Ask Questions

There are more questions than answers in life. But if you are not afraid to ask others about different things and about what you don't know or don't understand, then you will know more than someone who eschews questions. This daily practice is good for your self-development. Remember that the worst question is not the question asked. The habits of the rich cannot do without it.

Changing your habits, setting clear goals for yourself, drawing up a plan for their implementation, you will achieve financial success. The main thing is not to stop, but to go to your dream.

8

HOW TO INVEST YOUR MONEY IN 2020 AS A BEGINNER?

The question of why investing in various financial assets often arises for people who are just starting to be interested in ways of passive earnings. We can say that this skill belongs to the mandatory skills of a person who wants to succeed.

Another thing is that the vast majority of people spend almost all of their money on daily expenses - food, clothing, rents, and often also loans. This is a kind of dependence on the bank, state, place of work. And professionalism in one area or another is not a guarantee of good profit.

Why is it so important to support yourself financially?

Every person in the modern world just needs to learn how to manage their finances and increase them. Almost everyone periodically thinks about accumulating and achieving financial freedom, ensuring a comfortable old age, and investing in the future of their children.

A certain role is played by the state, giving older adults a pension from a pension fund, in which the amount of deductions from wages for life is accumulated. However, the size of pensions is well known to everyone - it is simply impossible to provide decent old age for them. Most pensioners who have worked all their lives live on the brink of poverty.

Why invest?

Why is the situation different in developed countries? Older people travel around the world and live life to the fullest. And these are not celebrities or oligarchs - these are ordinary average people.

The response is obvious around us based on what we can see in developed countries; investment plays a huge role in the life of the population. Up to 80% of Americans make investments in shares of large companies and receive dividends on them.

The question of why to invest is not raised there - they start investing at a young age. Just look at the numbers: in the USA, the volume of investments in investment funds is twice as much as the volume of bank deposits. The investor gets the opportunity to receive dividends from shares - investment income, which, in the future, can be several times higher than wages.

I hope that now it has become clearer to you why you need to invest. Firstly, this is a mandatory skill for every person who wants to strengthen their future and present financial situation. Secondly, it benefits the economy.

In addition, income from investments that exceed salaries in volume is not a fairy tale, but real statistics. And do not think that only wealthy and influential people become investors. It is within the power of every person right now. For example, in mutual funds, you can invest from one thousand. The choice is yours - to invest this thousand in the case or order rolls in the evening for the same amount.

WHAT YOU NEED BEFORE YOU START INVESTING

Before you start investing money, it will be useful to get acquainted with the advice of people who have reached sky-high peaks in the financial world and have already managed to write down their names in history.

Action:

Bill Gates once said that most people are not able to achieve their financial goals, not because of their intellectual or physical insolvency, but because they are wasting their time and energy. Engaged in routine and monotonous work, they kill their potential, but for some reason, continue to hope for success in the form of an inheritance from a long-forgotten relative or winning the lottery. Moreover, if they spent less on ordinary entertainment and invested more, then after 5–10 years they would have the opportunity to quit their disgusting work and do more interesting things.

Discipline:

This habit must be developed as early as possible and maintained throughout life. The development of discipline will allow you to control your expenses and consistently go to the goal no matter what. For example, Harold Hunt, the richest oilman of the 50s, came to work until the last in an old car and ate simple homemade food that he brought with him in a paper bag. Warren Buffett, even earning the first billion, continued to live in a house bought in 1958 for $31,500.

The essence of this advice is that everyone who is looking for real investment success should have the willpower to maintain the standard of living that corresponds to their income level. Loss of discipline will turn into a desire to thoughtlessly spend what you earn, which will inevitably lead to collapse.

Perseverance:

The path to investment success is a continuous series of ups and downs. The stories of large people in business who invested millions in stocks and squandered everything in one fell swoop often flicker as an example for beginner investors. But do not be afraid to invest, and even more so to give up this business after the first failures. Priceless experience comes with them, and investing little by little in different projects, the investor is unlikely to remain unprofitable.

Hence, experienced investors know that money lying in a "three-liter jar" on a shelf or under a mattress is the most unprofitable way to "invest." Banknotes and coins should be in constant motion, multiply, and work for its owner. Of course, there are risks that the investment project will fail, but if you approach the issue of investments correctly and carefully, you can always minimize these probabilities. What types of investments are there? Beginning investors should know the basic aspects of the competent distribution of capital.

As I've previously stated, the essence of investment is to invest capital (tangible or intangible) in various investment projects, securities, funds to make a profit in the future. Very often, some types of investments are compared with speculation; however, these are two different concepts. Indeed, speculative projects involve investing money for a period of up to one year (most often for a month or two).

All investments for more than a year are already investments. But there are types of investments that fall under these two definitions, such as operations on stock exchanges. They are mostly short-term in nature, but they are not called speculation.

3 MAIN AREAS OF INVESTMENT

Real investment:

This type of investment differs from others in that money is invested in real things: enterprises, privatized objects, real estate. There are several types of real investment:

Material: the creation of enterprises, investment in the expansion of production, or turnover.

Intangible: when money is invested in staff development, brand or trademark promotion, market research, advertising, design of a trading floor, etc.

How to Determine the Profitability of Investments?

You can use the dynamic method to assess the effectiveness of investments: determining the return on investment index, internal rate of return, or using the net present value method. Most often, they use the comparison method when the actual project is compared with a similar one, and the profit rate is determined. If it turns out to be high, then the investment is considered effective.

It is worth noting that such investments are considered risky; therefore, they require professional management. Before deciding on investments, for example, in a specific product, it is recommended to get the opportunity to influence the management of the company, and it is best to own the main stake.

There are cases when the management of the company and the investor did not agree on the methods of distributing investment funds. As a result, conflict situations arose. Proper management of real investments involves constant analysis of the market, the search for consensus between interested parties, and the forecasting of performance.

Features of Real Investment

Unlike the national currency, the rate of which can jump up and down, the objects of real investment are rarely depreciated. For example, an investor bought an apartment to rent it out, and it is only growing in price against the backdrop of general inflation. The rate of return on those kinds of investments is quite high. This is not a fixed percentage in the bank, as in the case of a deposit, but the opportunity to earn much more. After all, engaging in the expansion of production, modernization, staff development, you can get more quality products, and therefore more money.

But there are certain risks of this type of investment:

Technological progress affects the rapid loss of relevance to particular equipment. Real objects require constant investment. The investor is introducing new technologies, and the competitor has already acquired something even more high- tech.

Some real investment objects have low liquidity. For example, purchased raw materials quickly deteriorated, or equipment became outdated. In the latter case, financial instruments look more attractive. They can be easily sold on any exchange. But it is a real investment that allows the business to grow, operate more widely and efficiently.

Real Investment for Individuals

These types of investments do not require registration of a large number of securities (with the exception of investments in opening your own company):

Purchase of an apartment, house, or other premises for further rental. A very profitable investment is the purchase of an immovable object in a house under construction and its subsequent sale after putting the house into operation at a much higher price.

The acquisition of various equipment to lease or resell it at a better price.

Purchase of antiques, which only grows in price over time. Opening your own company.

Legal entities also use all these types of real investments, but the list of their opportunities is more extensive. It also includes modernization of production, reconstruction of buildings, construction of new facilities, and infrastructure equipment.

Financial Investment

This type of investment is considered the most popular and widespread. In this case, the investor uses various investment instruments to make a profit. In addition, a similar method can be used to diversify risks, gain control over the issuing company, and preserve capital. The main qualities of financial investment:

• accessibility for all types of investors;

• circulation in the secondary market;

• portfolio investment form available;

• high-level volatility;

• profitability is potentially high;

• the process is regulated by law.

Of course, there are risks of a decrease in profitability and loss of investment capital, but this is inherent in any type of investment.

Investment Process

How is the structure of financial investments distributed by markets?

- Currency - implies trading on FOREX, buying options for the further acquisition of the foreign currency, etc.
- Credit - the purchase of government or corporate securities, bonds, and other debt securities.
- Stock - purchase/sale of shares of various corporations and enterprises.

What Types of Financial Investments Are There?

Shares are considered the most highly profitable, but also a risky instrument. Bonds are usually backed by the state and are less risky but also less profitable. Mutual investment funds are considered to be a cross between the two previous investment instruments because, in this case, the money is controlled by professionals, which reduces the risk of losses. The financial type of investment also includes investments in precious metals, futures, options, forwards, depository receipts.

How Are Financial Investments Evaluated?

An analysis is being carried out (it is better to delegate these actions to specialists), taking into account external and internal data. The economy and condition of a particular financial sector, the forecast for the exchange rate of currencies and stocks are studied, and management and financial reporting are analyzed.

Determining the effectiveness of financial investments. Investments that allow funds to grow steadily are considered optimal and successful. An economic evaluation of effectiveness includes such methods: calculation of the payback period, internal and estimated rates of return, determination of net worth, and assessment of return on investment.

If we take into account all the results obtained, then we can choose the most suitable financial investment instrument.

It is worth noting that in addition to making a profit, this type of investment allows companies to strengthen their influence on the current market segment. Economists recommend forming an investment portfolio of different types of financial investments. This may be, for example, stock purchases, deposits, and currency. If the bank goes bankrupt, then there will still be stocks and currency.

Smart Investment

This type of investment involves investing in intangible products. Intellectual property may be private or collective. Objects for attachments:

- copyright patents;
- property of an informational nature (knowledge, experience, useful ideas);
- licensed property (the right to use goods and services secured by a license);
- purchase of scientific and technical products (information software, know-how).

The objects of intellectual investment can be technological, technical, or artistic. The latter, for example, include a previously unused design solution for a trademark or logo. For technical - improvement of equipment, mechanisms, and devices. Buying innovative software is also a way to invest.

This type of investment today is considered promising, but it also carries many risks. After all, no one will guarantee that the acquired technology, for example, will be successful in production.

However, the rapid development of the market simply forces us to look for new projects and ways to improve the business, so investment in intellectual property is very relevant. The creation of special exchanges that trade assets only confirms this fact. Intelligent investments are capable of making a "breakthrough" in the manufacturing sector with average financial injections. Such investments have a beneficial effect on the entire economy of the country as a whole.

It is very difficult to assess the effectiveness of this type of investment because even experienced experts are not able to predict the success of an intellectual project. But investors with a certain degree of adventurism still take risks and, in most cases, remain the winners.

Separation of Investment by Risk and Return

A conservative type of portfolio investment involves investing in bonds and government stocks. It is not necessary to wait for special incomes here; however, the risks are minimized. Diversified investments are based on sharing the degree of risk between different financial investment instruments, where the high profitability of some is insured by the reliability of others. The profitability of such a portfolio is equal to the average market indicator.

A conservative approach is inherent in investors who do not like risks. A moderate investment strategy involves the use of an equal share of risk-free and highly profitable "dangerous" investments with high liquidity. An aggressive way to manage your investment portfolio is to get as many incomes as possible. But in this case, the risks are very high, because the portfolio is formed from the shares of "green" companies, which have not yet gained credibility in the market, but are developing rapidly, as well as from new startups.

What Types of Investments Are Most Popular Today?

Bank deposit: This investment method is more familiar but not very profitable. The risks here are very low because deposits are insured, and if the bank collapses, then depositors will receive compensation.

The property: In some countries, over the past two years, prices for apartments, houses, or commercial premises have increased by 30%. But the lack of diversification, the cost of maintaining an immovable property in good condition, and low liquidity are significant disadvantages of this type of investment.

Investing in exchange-traded funds (ETFs): Although this market in our country is not yet very developed, it is considered promising. The low cost of ETFs (3-5 thousand), the possibility of currency diversification, and the high liquidity of such investments make them very profitable today. Buying an ETF involves investing immediately in several companies or in foreign organizations, which reduces the risks.

Investments in mutual funds are considered low-risk but require costs in the form of commissions for managers. However, relatively high dividends compensate for this drawback.

Bonds: This is a classic investment tool that has been popular for decades. The high yield here can provide long-term securities.

Hype projects: Although such investments are equivalent to sitting on a barrel of gunpowder, this is a very quick way to earn money. In a year, it is quite possible to double or even triple your capital. Experts do not recommend limiting themselves to just one hype, but to disperse money over several promising projects.

Modern people are actively investing in the stock market, which allows you to act in several directions at once, invest their money in stocks, and traditionally in gold. This type of investment, such as the purchase of cryptocurrency, has become very popular recently. The frantic jumps in the Bitcoin exchange rate caused a stir around it. The forecasts in this regard are very different - some are sure that the future will be with this kind of money, and that cryptocurrency will only go up, while others say that this is another bubble that will burst in the near future.

What Risks Are Inherent in Different Types of Investments

Risks are the probability of losing your capital due to specific events or for objective reasons. They can be of several types: market ones, occurring for reasons independent of the investor (reforms, crisis, legislative changes), and nonmarket ones that arise within the same company or organization (shortcomings in the business plan, force majeure).

Varieties of Market Risks:

Inflation: Thanks to it, interest rates on loans are rising, citizens' funds are depreciating, prices are rising. Inflation affects all market players, reducing real income. As a result, the payback period of investment projects is growing, and almost all profits are "eaten up" by an increase in the circulation of paper money in the country.

Political risks: Any more or less influential event in the political field can "come back" to investors. The adoption of various regulations and legislative amendments indirectly affects some types of investments.

Economic nuances: Tax rates are rising, the key rate of the Central Bank is growing, and interest on loans is growing. Such aspects cannot but affect the investment. Costs of investors increase profit decreases along with an increase in the payback period of the project.

There are also currency risks when fluctuations affect the attractiveness of projects for investors. Therefore, it is recommended to invest in several types of currencies at once. Non-market risks include credit, personal, liquid, niche, and managerial risks.

Nevertheless, a novice investor should trust the specialists in selecting the optimal method and type of investment. Experts will help you in choosing a strategy, tell you where you can make good money, and which projects are best avoided.

Of course, you can do without outside help, if we are talking about small amounts of deposits. But if investing is the main source of income, then it's not worth the risk.

Financial advisors or managers in mutual funds will help to "make" good money. However, the availability of economic knowledge does not hurt.

What Is the Importance of Learning Before Investing?

It is particularly important to train to invest. Taking action without having trained often pays cash (in every sense of the word, moreover!). Training, it may seem boring, it is sometimes expensive. However, training is essential, whatever the field.

Let's see why.

Mistakes linked to lack of knowledge and skills

Why is training before investing important? Simply because you run the risk of making mistakes by doing things without mastering them. And because these mistakes can be expensive. In the stock market, bad choices or choices based on bad advice can melt most of a hard-won capital.

When we are aware that we do not know enough in one area, we have three choices:

- Act anyway while risking making big mistakes, a little in Tarzan Mode with the knife on your belt
- Call on an "expert" to advise us or to act on our behalf
- Take the time to form, by postponing the passage to action until the moment when we will sufficiently master the subject

TARZAN MODE: DOING THINGS WITHOUT TRAINING

The first choice is, depending on the area, sometimes without major long-term consequences (try a new dish without following a recipe, for example). But when it comes to investing, it's a pretty suicidal choice: if you're lucky, everything can go well. For a while, at least.

In real estate, for example, an error can cost tens of thou- sands of dollars, and impact your financing capacity (or even your capacity to honor your loan) for long years.

Call in an Expert

The second choice is to call on people who wear the expert's cap and ask them, either:

- Advice to guide us in our actions
- To act in our place

For example: ask your neighbor's cousin who has already invested in the stock market for advice or even goes and sees your banker says: "I save $250 / month, what can I do with it?"

The second choice may seem more sensible, but in terms of investment, it hides a very big trap. As much as it is better to go to a doctor when you are sick, as much as going to see a banker, a broker or a fund manager to invest is not the best thing to do.

Why? Because there is a conflict of interest between you and your banker/broker/investment fund. When a professional place your money, he is paid a percentage of your return. It seeks to make this percentage as high as possible, which is against your interest since the higher this commission, the less you will earn.

In addition, it has been demonstrated that a professional who places your money will obtain a lower return than the market most of the time (then if he takes more of your return, you are very badly embarked).

Your doctor, on the other hand, has no interest in you staying sick (well, he still has an interest in you getting sick from time to time, but none in not treating you or doing it the wrong way).

Take The Time to Train Before Investing

There remains the choice of training, a choice that requires making two concessions in the short term:

- Agree to postpone taking action over time
- Spend time, see money, acquire the necessary knowledge/skills

These two concessions will be counterbalanced in the long term by better results and/or by avoiding future problems.

For example, learning before starting work on a property will avoid having to do it again later for anything that has been badly done, and will thus save time and money.

Likewise, training before investing in the stock market will have long-term beneficial effects. For example, correctly assessing your risk tolerance level and clearly defining your investment objectives and timeframe will avoid having your capital melt by 50% the next time the market turns. And thus to avoid big stress and all the bad decisions which would result from it.

Training Often Seems Obvious

Who would have the idea of climbing a 100m high cliff without having followed climbing lessons? To try to repair your car without knowing anything about mechanics? Or even cross the Amazon jungle without being interested in survival techniques in a hostile environment?

In many areas, training seems obvious. In others, it is much less so. However, training is often just as useful in these other areas. Investment is no exception.

When you invest, the dangers are less predictable, but potentially just as devastating. Most people have no education on this issue. Yet everyone is handling the money, and many people are investing.

I will detail all that is involved to go through these three choices.

The guaranteed recipe for going from dead-end to dead-end

Invest without training

First Error: The Ego and The Illusion

Starting alone without training can lead you to make two mistakes. You can also find them quite coarse with hindsight today.

When you're looking for the awesome and little known technique that would make your fortune (the illusion). Some are tricked by binary options, or by fake trading sites based in tax havens that bar with customer money by escaping international regulations. Hence, you can be fooled by Forex, and mistakenly thought it was a viable system for getting rich.

You may be aware of not having enough knowledge in trading, but you still wanted to try it (The ego: "you never know, it can work for me!").

So when you decide to trade yourself partially and to delegate the choice of some of your positions to people supposedly very efficient to cover you. This is what social trading, or copy-trading, does.

You link your account to that of a trader that you think is performing, and your account automatically copies all the positions that the trader takes. You, therefore, realize the same gains (and the same losses) as him, in proportion to your initial investment.

When you choose not to train. So, not only do you not have the skills, but you don't master the processes, and you want to be dependent on another, as well as on a system that could evolve and change the rules at any time. In short, you're not master of your boat.

What happened? Well, as you can imagine, the positions quickly fell into the red. As for social trading, in addition to the many technical problems it encountered (positions not copied for unknown reasons ...), good traders are good until they are no longer, they cram their account and yours with.

By the way, Forex is a market open 24/7, in which traders spend their days monitoring their positions, which is nervously very demanding. In addition, they are in direct competition with trading robots that never tire and do not need a vacation. Suffice to say, no need to draw a picture of your chances of long-term success in this market.

Errors Upon Errors

The second error corresponds to the 2nd choice: call a professional.

Following this first disappointment in investment, when you decide to do like most people: trust the experts. For example, you invest in Life Insurance via a pilot fund. In this case, no need to be trained as in Forex. You just have to invest your money, and good fund managers promise great success for little cost.

Delegating to compensate for your lack of knowledge/skills implies that the expert to whom you delegate your investments is sufficiently competent, and that they do not charge you too much for their skills.

In this case, too, your results were wrong. The fund manager of your insurance generated a negative result, which made you regret, and in addition, you had to pay fees on these results. Damned!

Small aside: on the stock market, some rare investment funds outperform the market, even once the net of fees. However, these funds may no longer open to the public, or they are still open. Still, they require a minimum investment amount so large that they are inaccessible to ordinary people (and investors).

Here again, the lesson was harsh, but you'd understood one thing: you're solely responsible for these failures because you had never made an effort to train yourself properly. You can now decide to acquire all the knowledge necessary never again to have to depend on a system or a person who would make the choices for you.

So yes, training yourself has a high cost, both in money and time. Buy training, take the time to study. But this cost will always be lower than that of not having trained.

Abraham Lincoln said: "If education is expensive, try ignorance."

Training: The Path to Success

Your failures to learn in the first place will give you the energy and the impetus to get started in training. We remain human, and it should not be forgotten. We are emotional beings, and the one who succeeds in investing or in trading is not the one who controls his emotions the best, but the one who sets up in a system that will never cause emotional peaks that can be at the origin of bad decisions.

By training in this way, you've got the impression of having descended into the arena, of having tasted the earth and of having gone deep into understanding the investment. Combined with the establishment of a daily learning environment (reading excellent books, podcasts, expert video interviews), the seminar and the school will allow you to acquire both theory and practice. But also confidence by validating the main principles through experience.

How to Train Effectively to Invest?

So how do you train? By acquiring knowledge based on the experience of others via books, seminars, online, or face-to- face training. You can also find podcasts and lots of video content. Be careful though: YouTube is a jungle; I advise you not to base your investment decisions on this type of content. It is better to start with books or training, which will have much more structured content.

Then don't forget to put your knowledge into practice. Who to train with? It is generally advisable to train with people who have the highest degree of perceived expertise (It is sometimes difficult to assess a person's real expertise through an article or a video. We can, therefore, speak of perceived expertise), and the most results to present.

Be careful; however, the results must be qualified according to the field: If one wishes to train in advertising on social networks, a field that generates immediate results: it will be particularly important to consider the results of the trainer.

For investment, focused on the long term, a trainer can take several years before having significant results to present (substantial building stock or a large investment portfolio). We can then seek to assess the dynamics of the person's evolution rather than an absolute result.

In which world to form? In the academic and theoretical world or the professional world focused on practice? (In other words: learn yoga by reading the yoga bible and with the local teacher or from a renowned Yogi master). Intuitively, one could say: with the best, therefore from the practical world (and from the master Yogi).

So, it's best to learn from the "masters in the field," those who proved in the open that they excelled in practice, and who had built their strategy on the experience of a lifetime.

It is, however, interesting to seek to cross this knowledge with that of the great theoreticians, academics, or more modest professors, to see if the modes of thought meet, in what they diverge, and if it is possible to take advantage of the best of two worlds.

Next: Implementation

Knowledge without practice produces no results. You have to go through the application and implementation of what you know to approach the next step and gain enough experience.

When do you know you've gained enough experience? Quite simply when the results are there. As long as there are no results, it is because either knowledge or experience (and therefore practice) is lacking.

Continuous training or how to stay on top and also train to stay on top.

The finish line

Often, after implementing something that works, you may run the risk of saying, "I finally understood and learned this stuff. That is all I know now, I am satisfied with the results obtained, and I can let myself slide quietly on the river of life."

To think so is often a mistake because there is always some- thing that we do not yet know.

The goal is not to call into question all his achievements. On the contrary, you have to know how to capitalize on each new knowledge brick. This does not prevent wanting to add new ones by asking the question: "What do I not know yet?" "

I think there is no finish line when you train in a field. Our learning curve resembles a kind of asymptote which tends towards infinity without ever reaching it.

Asymptotic Investment Learning Curve

When you start learning something new, the curve starts to climb very high as you learn new things, then its growth slows down. It is logical, the more we know, the less there is to learn. Except that the limit is unattainable since it is impossible to know everything about everything: however, we can always learn new things.

It is a bit like a high-level tennis player, or a professional violin player in a philharmonic orchestra. Their room for improvement is very small compared to a novice in their field. But have they finished their apprenticeship yet? Oh no. Roger Federer continues to work his forehand, just like Yoda continues to train to master the force, even after his death.

If we observe the greatest champions in the sport, they never stop trying to progress. Because if they stop and start to believe that they have "arrived," then this will be the beginning of the end for them.

A Small Detail

Today I keep asking myself, " What don't I know?" " There is so much content available that it is always possible to go a little further on a specific point.

The more we understand, the more likely it is to come across content that we have already incorporated into our knowledge. In this case, it is not useless since we will be reinforced in his knowledge and his fundamentals (it's a bit like if Roger Federer's coach asks him to rework his forehand although he already masters it perfectly: the objective is also to maintain this level of mastery).

It also sometimes happens to come across a small nugget on a sentence, a small detail that will allow you to see certain things from another angle, which will allow you to improve a little more and to change a little something in your practice.

However, it is very improbable to be able to achieve your financial goals, independence, or financial freedom without having trained (whether in real estate, stock market, in creating a business and others).

We can never be fully aware of the knowledge we lack. When it comes to investing, there is one question that can help you assess a training need. This question is to ask yourself if you feel able to generate half a million dollars in wealth during your life, ideally when you are about to retire.

If you have already reached this age or are close to it, you can ask yourself another question: "Do you have or are you on the way to having a heritage of half a million dollars?"

Why this question, and why this figure in particular?

If you don't have at least half a million dollars in assets or wealth, or if you don't think you'll be able to accumulate similar capital by retirement age is that you lack knowledge, where you lacked it for part of your life.

Why? Because it is an amount that it is possible to generate during working life. Not only is it possible, but it is also rather easy and mechanical.

I will even go a little further, at the risk of shocking: the price of your ignorance is (or will be) the difference between this half a million and what you own (or what you think you will have at this age).

The question is quite rough; I am aware of it. However, it is not based on a random figure. This half a million corresponds to a reasonable amount of savings for an average employee, invested at a rate lower than that of historical stock market returns, all during working life, that is to say about 40 years. This amount can also correspond to the value of five apartments whose credits have been reimbursed, in an average city.

The two approaches that I have just mentioned to arrive at such a figure require some knowledge, and therefore training before investing. Because the cost of ignorance can turn out to be very expensive, much more expensive than anything you could spend to train yourself.

You should normally be convinced at this stage of the chapter that training is essential in investment as in other areas. Throughout a lifetime, this can make all the difference between spending happy, free, and carefree old days, and still looking for a job at 75, with a person's state of form.

And you, will you dare to ask yourself what you do not yet know? Do you already have a plan or training in mind to achieve your goals?

AFTERWORD

Imagine for a moment, and you have just written your goal, it seems within your reach. You start working on it to reach it. Yes, you believe in it, you will get there, that's for sure! But the results are long overdue; you start to despair; your motivation declines.

Then the urge to stop everything comes to your mind, and negative ideas start to arise in your mind; I'm not good at that, I would never get there, I aimed too high, it's too hard ... In short, you will be frustrated.

But you roll up your sleeves. No, you're not going to give up. You think that if this goal cannot be reached at the moment, well, it doesn't matter, and you choose one that seems more within your reach.

Then you start again with another goal, easier to reach. But the heart is not there anymore, your confidence in you begins to be reduced like the skin of sorrow. You begin to resign yourself and accept your current situation with sentences such as: "there are more people unhappy than me. I'm not bad like that, after all." You give up. What a pity.

There can be several reasons, but the main two are:

Either it is not yours. That is to say that it was either imposed on you or strongly recommended or simply blown. Your choice has been influenced.

Either it is too small. A goal must be great. Sometimes you want to achieve something, but it is a "nothing more" desire. It cannot be a goal. Indeed, a goal must be very motivating to be able to achieve it. A goal is a dream to achieve.

In this book, I've been able to highlight some of the best approaches to erase debts while increasing your wealth with the almost unknown rule used by the rich. Also, it is worth noting that happiness is not completely related to money. In some cases, money can make people happy, but money and happiness are not linked. It is clear that if we did not have money, we could not live. But it doesn't make money more important than your family. If you destroy your financial situation, you will have a feeling of great sorrow; on the other hand, if you destroy your family, you will have nobody. In this case, the negative side of money is completely real. Money problems remain unpleasant, but they can always be resolved.

When you have trouble paying your rent, providing for the family, or funding the care of a loved one, you feel bad, and it's okay. All these money-created disabilities cause us sorrow, and we could feel bad. You must avoid depressing for lack of money because you could still fix things and set the record straight.

From what you've learned in this guide are the amazing ways to manage your budget and get your head out of the water.

Remember, to know how to manage your money and get rich, and it's very simple. The first thing to do is think about your sources of income. How many do you have that make you money? How much money do you earn every month? Many people do not know how much is falling on their bank account. They receive their payslips without understanding how the salary was assessed. You can steal money from them, and they'll never know. Before looking for solutions to manage your money well, it is important to know what you earn. You had to know the exact amount to the nearest penny.

If you only have one source and it's solid enough for you to live the life of your dreams, that's fine. On the other hand, if it is not enough to live and save, it is high time to find others to help you.

What are the main obstacles that prevent you from achieving your goals?

Fear

We are afraid of not succeeding, so we set ourselves small goals so that we can reach them more easily, and we miss them. Why? Because these little goals don't motivate you enough, they don't get you into action. Fear prevents you from getting what you want in your life.

The chances of the future are more and more important, immense fortunes have been made over the last 15 years (Facebook, Google, Amazon ...) Previously fortunes were made over several generations. But today's successes are very rapid. So why have such a narrow vision and a great fear of the future? You have to change your mentality and acquire a winning mentality as rightly stated about the habit of the rich in Chapter 7 of this guide.

See Too Small

You can't motivate yourself by dreaming of a holiday at the Blue Flots campsite and taking a pedal boat ride on Lake Annecy. It is certainly pleasant as a vacation, but are you ready to work twice as much and to divide your lifestyle by two to offer it to you? See, the motivation is largely insufficient.

Focus On What You Want

Do you know what you want? Have you decided what you wanted to do with your life? It is your responsibility; no one can do it for you. Decide what you want and put the focus on it, that is, think about what you want and forget what you don't want. Our dominant thoughts create our life. If you continually think about what you want to avoid, then you're going to attract it.

Sow Your Goal in Your Mind and Let It Take Root

How do you sow what you want in your mind? It's quite simple, and for some, it even seems simplistic. What a shame to believe this because, in reality, it is of phenomenal power. You have to make positive affirmations. When you think of a goal, you have to pretend you have already achieved it.

You have to let it germinate. What does it mean to let it germinate? It means letting it take root. Do not dig up the seed you just planted; otherwise, it will never grow. If you change your mind like a shirt, the seed doesn't have time to develop and come up with a wonderful flower. So give time to time. Just as a plant needs time to grow, a thought needs time to manifest in the world.

Don't Confuse

Do not start to doubt the possibility of success. "I don't know if I'm going to get there" is really out of your vocabulary. "I will try," too! We don't try! We do ... or we don't, but we don't try. You must be in a feeling of certainty. You know you have taken the right path, the one that suits you today. Go ahead, go for it, and realize it.

Let Go of Your Past

The past is past, and the future has not yet arrived, so focus on the present moment. You must be present in what you are doing to be much more efficient and more attentive to what is going on inside you. Indeed, in you, it moves! Listen.

Listen to your body, listen to your mind, speak to you, be attentive, be in the present moment. Expect to succeed even better than you think. Beyond your expectations. You deserve the best.

Take Responsibility for Your Life

I have good news and bad news.

The bad news is that you are responsible for your current situation. It was created by your thoughts of yesterday. You know the saying, "we reap what we sow." You sowed negative thoughts, and therefore today, you are reaping.

The good news is that there are actually two.

The first is that you have "purged" some of these negative thoughts. Since you have experienced difficulties, these are about to end because of the negative karma, which you had created goes out. The second good news is that you are responsible for your future. Your thoughts of today create your future.

Who is the "authority" over your thoughts? There is only one: YOU. Indeed, no one can force you to think this or that.

Now you can set up a formidable system to reach them. You are going to measure your progress because you cannot afford to sail on sight for the success of your life.

And now ...

In the past, you had desired. You wanted to earn more, erase your debts, buy a house ... But today, you have goals. You have them clearly defined. You know what you want, so be on the go all the time. Don't wait for things to happen ... provoke them!

Come On, Take Action.

Having a reserve of money makes you feel secure. You must, therefore, learn to control your finances before they can control you!

RESOURCES

Alux.com. (2019). 15 Habits of RICH & Successful People. Retrieved from https://www.youtube.com/watch?v=-yD5Mj0UIIw

Ankit Garg. (2020). How to Set Financial Goals and Actually Meet Them. Retrieved from https://www.lifehack.org/articles/money/ditch-the-excuses-15-tips-quit-spending-your-money.html

ARIELLE O'SHEA. (2020). How to Invest in Real Estate: 5 Ways to Get Started. Retrieved from https://www.nerdwallet.com/blog/investing/5-ways-to-invest-in-real-estate/

Atrill, P. (2009). Financial Management for Decision Makers. 5th ed. Harlow England: Pearson Education Limited, p.136.

Betterment Boss. (2019). 7 Hacks to Save Money on A Low Income | How to Save Money Fast on a Low Income. Retrieved from https://www.youtube.com/watch?v=zUYJg6rhHjY

Brian Tracy. (2020). Subconscious Mind Power Explained. Retrieved from https://www.briantracy.com/blog/personal-success/understanding-your-subconscious-mind/

BRIANNA MCGURRAN & ARIELLE O'SHEA. (2020). How to Start Investing: A Guide for Beginners. Retrieved from https://www.nerdwallet.com/blog/investing/how-to-start- investing/

Brianna Wiest. (2018). 13 Ways to Start Training Your Subconscious Mind to Get What You Want. Retrieved from https://www.forbes.com/sites/briannawiest/2018/09/12/ 13-ways-to-start-training-your-subconscious-mind-to-get- what-you-want/#7ae0b2867d69

Candice Elliott. (2019). Want to Know How to Become Rich? Here Are 21 Interesting Habits of Rich People. Retrieved from https://www.listenmoneymatters.com/how-to-become-rich/

Cary Siegel. (2013). Why Didn't They Teach Me This in School?: 99 Personal Money Management Principles to Live By. New Edition. California, US. Createspace Independent Publishing Platform. p.100-150.

Chelsea Brennan. (2020). Good Debt Vs. Bad Debt. Retrieved from https://www.forbes.com/advisor/loans/good-debt-vs-bad-debt/

Chris Mettler. (2017). Unexpected Effects of Poor Money Management. Retrieved from https://www.huffpost.com/ entry/unexpected-effects-of-poo_b_7820962

Chris Schoonover. (2020). Ditch The Excuses: 15 Tips To Quit Spending Your Money. Retrieved from https://www. lifehack.org/articles/money/ditch-the-excuses-15-tips-quit-spending-your-money.html

Dave Ramsey. (2020). How to Save Money: 20 Simple Tips. Retrieved from https://www.daveramsey.com/blog/the-secret-to-saving-money

Dave Ramsey. (2013). The Total Money Makeover: Classic Edition: A Proven Plan for Financial Fitness. Classic Edition. New York, US. Thomas Nelson. p.50

Dr. Joseph Murphy, Ian McMahan (2001). The Power of Your Subconscious Mind. New Edition. New York, US. Bantam Books. p.45-60

EileenOShanassy. (2017). 5 Consequences of Managing Money Unwisely. Retrieved from https://menaentrepreneur. org/2017/07/5-consequences-of-managing-money- unwisely/

ERIC WHITESIDE, Reviewed By MARGUERITA CHENG. (2020). What Is the 50/20/30 Budget Rule?. Retrieved from https://www.investopedia.com/ask/answers/022916/what-502030-budget-rule.asp

FindLaw's team of legal writers and editors. (2018). Tips for Avoiding Debt. Retrieved from https://bankruptcy.findlaw. com/debt-relief/tips-for-avoiding-debt.html

Kiyosaki, R. T., & Lechter, S. L. (1998). Rich dad, poor dad: What the rich teach their kids about money that the poor and middle class do not!. Paradise Valley, Ariz: TechPress. p.10.

Marko - WhiteBoard Finance. (2019). How To Manage Your Money (50/30/20 Rule). Retrieved from https://www. youtube.com/watch?v=HQzoZfc3GwQ

Marko - WhiteBoard Finance. (2019). How To Pay OffDebt (Debt Snowball vs. Debt Avalanche).

Retrieved from https://www.youtube.com/watch?v=pftx9Jx6N1Q

Michelle and Beverly Bertram. (2013). 10 Principles of Money Mastery. Retrieved from https://www.foxbusiness. com/features/10-principles-of-money-mastery

PAULA PANT. (2020). 7 Habits That Will Help You Pay off Debt. Retrieved from https://www.thebalance.com/habits- to-pay-off-debt-4125554

PAULA PANT REVIEWED BY MARGUERITA CHENG.
(2020). The 50/30/20 Rule of Thumb for Budgeting: Eliza- beth Warren's 50/30/20 rule can help you manage your budget. Retrieved from https://www.thebalance.com/the- 50-30-20-rule-of-thumb-453922

Rianka Dorsainvil. (2019). Does Your Budget Feel Scary?. Retrieved from
https://www.forbes.com/sites/ riankadorsainvil/2019/10/30/does-your-budget-feel- scary/#3c383b6c7774

Robert Farrington. (2018). 10 IMPORTANT REASONS EVERYONE SHOULD LEARN HOW TO INVEST.
Retrieved from https://thecollegeinvestor.com/10993/10- reasons-everyone-should-learn-how-to-invest-6-is-my-favorite-reason/

Sean Pyles. (2018). How to Avoid Debt in 3 Simple Steps. Retrieved from https://www.nerdwallet.com/blog/finance/ how-to-avoid-debt/

Sherrie Haynie. (2020). Building A Better Money Management Strategy With The Power Of Personality Type. Retrieved from https://www.forbes.com/sites/forbescoachescouncil/2020/02/13/building-a-better- money-management-strategy-with-the-power-of- personality-type/#384b87b52729

Stephanie Steinberg and Susannah Snider. (2019). 10 Easy

Ways to Pay Off Debt. Retrieved from https://money.usnews.com/money/personal-finance/debt/articles/easy-ways-to-pay-off-debt

Trent Hamm. (2018). 22 Ways to Reduce Your Spending Without Making Your Life Miserable. Retrieved from https://www.thesimpledollar.com/save-money/21-ways-to-reduce-your-spending-without-making-your-life- miserable/

Trent Hamm. (2020). How to Save Money Fast. Retrieved from https://www.thesimpledollar.com/save-money/little-steps-100-great-tips-for-saving-money-for-those-just-getting-started/

Jamelle Sanders. (2014). Unleash the Power of Your Mind!. Retrieved from https://www.huffpost.com/entry/unleash- the-power-of-your_1_b_5964592

Jeff Rose. (2016). The 15 Crucial Steps Needed To Achieve Financial Independence. Retrieved from https://www.forbes.com/sites/jrose/2016/03/25/financial-independence/#1795eda4984b

Printed by Libri Plureos GmbH in Hamburg, Germany